THE UNVEILING...

THE UNVEILING...

Monty Stratton, D. Min.
Foreword by Brad Herrin

FOUNDATION MINISTRIES INTERNATIONAL

8703 GAYTON RD.

RICHMOND, VA 23229

PHONE: (804) 754-3811

E-MAIL: foundationministries@fm-i.org

WEBSITE: www.fm-i.org

Unless otherwise noted, scripture quotations are taken from the King James Version of the Bible.

ISBN: 0-9666648-0-9

Printed in the United States of America

Dedication

I would like to dedicate this book, first and foremost, to my Lord Jesus. This is His revelation, which I have been entrusted to share with you. The passion for a company of sons in His image released this revelation in the secret place. As my head and listening ear reclined on His breast, He shared with me the unveiling of Himself, unwrapping the mystery of the ages – **CHRIST IN YOU, THE HOPE OF GLORY!**

Secondly, I would like to dedicate this book to all the saints who have been misunderstood and rejected because they didn't fit the religious molds of the time. Religion focuses on programs, but the Kingdom of God focuses on a Person. His name is Jesus! Those of you marked for the Kingdom of God will never be satisfied with the spiritual status quo. It is to you that *The Unveiling...* is dedicated.

Acknowledgments

*T*o Brad Herrin, a faithful scribe in the Kingdom, for spending many hours relentlessly proof-reading and editing this book with a spirit of excellence.

To my family, for yielding many hours of my personal time spent in the secret place, because they knew the Lord was revealing His glory, to be unveiled in the Church.

To an unnamed brother in the Lord, for hearing and obeying the Master's voice and providing the financial means for *The Unveiling...* to become a reality.

Foreword

*A*s an avid reader of good books, I am happily surprised to come across the rare gem that stirs spirit, soul, and body. Such books are marked by the breath of the Spirit of God and arrive at such a time that life and fellowship with the Lord are permanently altered. The book that you now hold has become such a rare gem to me, and, I am confident that it will prove to be so, for all those whom the Spirit has prepared to receive it.

As the author states in this book, God works in different ways at different times. God's revelation is progressive and this book is a step forward into the mind and will of God for the present time. If you are willing to follow the glory cloud when it moves and to abide when it rests, you will find this book to be a welcome companion on your way. In it you will find the answer to why the Lord has led you through wilderness ways, and you will catch a glimpse of the glory that lies ahead.

Be prepared to be startled at times by the Lord's revelation. He is, after all, an awesome God, and we should expect awesome revelations from Him. Even as John was overwhelmed by the revelation given to him, we should anticipate to be prostrated in awe and worship of One so great and mighty, One who delights to give good gifts to His children.

Recently, I had prayed that the Lord would reveal to me any beliefs I held that were not from

Him. In response, He sent me this book. I supposed that the Lord would rearrange some stones that were placed way up on the wall of my life; I had no idea He would reach down so close to the foundation to begin His work. However, because the work was foundational, it has set everything that rests upon it on a more sure base. The house is now more solid than it was, and it can now rise much higher.

I trust that you will be surprised, even as I was, that there is so much more to this Christian life than what is commonly anticipated. No more need we abide in the "wretched man that I am" mindset, for our God is transforming us "from glory to glory." The Lord is coming a third and final time to cleanse the temple and then His glory will fill it, this time to abide forever, nevermore to leave. Oh glorious thought, WE ARE THAT TEMPLE!

Brad Herrin

Contents

INTRODUCTION

*J*ust as the children of Issachar understood the times in which they lived (I Chronicles 12:32), we also as the body of Christ are to understand the times in which we live. The apostle Peter spoke of this when he stated we were to be established in present truth (I Peter 1:12). As Spirit-filled believers, we need to be established with wisdom and balance.

Present truth gives us perspective. The written Word and the spoken Word together provide a confirming witness, establishing the counsel of God for the hour in which we live. The written Word (logos) gives us a foundation of principles from the Lord Himself, as a cornerstone of our walk with Him. The spoken Words (rhema) are revelation stones, or heavenly patterns, we receive from the Holy Spirit. When the truths hidden in the written Word (logos) are personally revealed to us by the Holy Spirit, they become flesh. Present truth gives our walk purpose, with a vision of our destiny. Psalms 119:105 gives us this balanced viewpoint: "THY WORD IS A LAMP UNTO MY FEET, AND A LIGHT UNTO MY PATH."

We must have fresh revelation from heaven which is grounded in the written Word of God in order to bring forth a manifestation (revelation) of God in us, then through us, that we might be established in this generation. Two important foundation stones must be laid to prepare us to receive the breath of revelation from God. The first foundation stone is that God wants to reveal Himself, in these last days, by His Spirit. The second is that this revelation will be in the form of type and pattern, as seen by those who seek Him (II Chronicles 28:12, 19; Mark 4:34). They are found in the following passages of scripture:

> But as it is written, eye hath not seen, nor ear heard, neither have entered into the heart of man, the things which God hath prepared for them that love Him. But God hath revealed them unto us by His Spirit: For the Spirit searcheth all things, yea the deep things of God...Which things also we speak, not in the words which man's wisdom teacheth, but which the Holy Ghost teacheth; comparing spiritual things with spiritual...Now we have received not the spirit of the world, but the Spirit which is of God: that we might know the things that are freely given to us of God. (I Corinthians 2:9-10, 13, 12)
>
> But there is a God in heaven that revealeth secrets...He revealeth the deep and secret things. (Daniel 2:28, 22)
>
> Deep calleth unto deep at the noise of Thy water spouts. (Psalms 42:7)
>
> And let them make Me a sanctuary; that I may dwell among them. According to all that I shew thee, after the pattern of the tabernacle. (Exodus 25:8-9)
>
> For, see, saith He, that thou maketh all things according to the pattern shewed to thee in the mount. (Hebrews 8:5)

The purpose of this book is to blow a trumpet in Zion, announcing that God's Holy Spirit is brooding over the deep in His servants. There is a cry ascending to the Father from all over this land as God's people are getting on their faces before Him. In response, a voice from heaven is coming forth saying, "The Kingdom of God is within you" (Luke 17:21). The unveiling is upon us!

He instructed me to allow my mouth to become a pen as of a ready writer, to trumpet in Zion the time of the Glory of the Kingdom is at hand. The unveiling is becoming a present reality in the people of God, His church. We have not been this way before. The Pentecostal/Charismatic renewal was one of outward focus of the manifestations of the gifts of the Spirit (words of knowledge, healings, and prophecy). This renewal will bring the balance of an inward focus of revelation and fruit. The blending of the two will result in a balanced manifestation of Jesus Christ in us, and therefore in our world.

> According as His divine power hath given unto us all things that pertain unto life and godliness, through the knowledge of Him that hath called us to glory and virtue: Whereby are given unto us exceeding great and precious promises: that by these ye might be partakers of the divine nature, having escaped the corruption that is in the world through lust. (II Peter 1:3, 4)

That which was from the beginning, which we have heard, which we have seen with our eyes, which we have looked upon, and our hands have handled, of the Word of life; (for the life was manifested, and we have seen it, and bear witness, and shew unto you that eternal life, which was with the Father, and was manifested unto us;) that which we have seen and heard declare we unto you, that ye also may have fellowship with us: and truly our fellowship is with the Father, and with His son Jesus Christ. (I John 1:1-3)

Many are hearing a whisper coming from the depths of their heart, the sanctuary of God, saying, "Come up hither and I will show you things to come" (Rev. 4:1). The throne of God in you is providing an open vision into the restorational patterns and processes, unveiling the Christ in you to this last generation. Our response as the Church needs to be, "Amen!"

This is our finest hour. Jesus has saved the best for last. The scripture, "as He is, so are we in this world" (I John 4:17b), is being fulfilled. May we be like John the beloved, placing our head on Jesus' breast, to receive a revelation of His heart.

The Unveiling... is the first volume of a restoration trilogy. As you read it, my prayer is that God will be glorified and your joy may be full as you become the expression of Christ in the earth. The whole creation is groaning, waiting for the manifestation of the sons of God, to manifest the Son of God.

Monty Stratton, D.Min.

UNIT I
The Destiny of God—A Prophetic Perspective

CHAPTER ONE

The Hourglass of the Tabernacle

Since we have discovered that God has a destiny for us and placed the deposit of eternity in our hearts, then how will God bring perspective and focus into our private worlds?

Once God has apprehended us and given us the gift of repentance, something wonderful happens! He begins to align our hearts' desires with His, for the express purpose of coming into agreement with His will.

How does God bring His perspective to pass? Is it an instant transformation in our lives? Do we wake up one morning to the realization that we are clothed with God's glory, and manifesting the life of His Son, Jesus?

The Lord planned from eternity to bring His eternal perspective into focus, which is to be walked out by each of us. Therefore, our heavenly Father established a witness of two things, in order to bring us to full maturity and completion. These two things are times and patterns. The Bible gives some wonderful reflections concerning times (or timing) and patterns.

> To everything there is a season, and a time to every purpose, under the heaven...He hath made everything beautiful in His time...For there is a time there for every purpose and for every work. (Ecclesiastes 3:1, 11, 17)

See, saith He, that thou make all things according to the pattern shewed to thee in the mount. (Hebrews 8:5)

According to all that I shew thee, after the pattern of the tabernacle ... let them make Me a sanctuary; that I may dwell among them. (Exodus 25:9, 8)

A minister of the sanctuary, and of the true tabernacle, which the Lord pitched and not man. (Hebrews 8:2)

It was therefore necessary that the patterns of things in the heavens should be purified with these ... for Christ is not entered into the holy places made with hands, which are the figures of the true; but into heaven itself, now to appear in the presence of God for us. (Hebrews 9:23, 24)

God is intimately involved in the affairs of men. He gives us heavenly patterns over time, leading us to a place called perfection. We discover these heavenly patterns as we observe His intimate involvement in our lives. It is in the trademark, the unique imprint that reveals the designer's pattern. The signature comes with His character, nature, and perspective all woven into the fabric.

The best illustration to see this demonstrated is with Jesus Himself in the tabernacle. When we go back and review the tabernacle of Moses, with its distinctive rooms, furniture, and functions; we are awed by the reality that Jesus' life embodied every phase. We see Christ's progression from sacrificial lamb in the outer court to king/priest in the Most Holy Place. The scriptures in Hebrews confirm that Jesus indeed walked out the

Father's perspective, in order to become the pattern Son.

In addition, Jesus had a proper focus. He understood the patterns and timing. He had a spirit likened unto the children of Issachar. He walked with a corresponding focus of heavenly patterns, being revealed and released at the right time. I love an example of this in His life, found in John 13:3-5.

> Jesus KNOWING that the Father had given all things into His hands, and that He was come from God, and went to God; He riseth from supper, and laid aside His garments; and took a towel, and girded Himself. After that He poureth water into a basin, and began to wash the disciples' feet, and to wipe them with the towel wherewith He was girded.

He had the *knowing* (the revealed perspective) from the Father. He was secure in that loving intimate knowledge of who He was, where He had come from, and where He was going. This intimacy provided Him with patterns and timing, allowing Him to walk out God's perfect will. God is calling each of us to intimacy with Him, which progressively reveals:

1. PERSPECTIVE - to BE His will in the earth.
2. FOCUS - to DO of His good pleasure.

Many Christians today are running around with a misguided focus. They are doing a lot of seemingly good works, but missing the mark because they lack God's perspective. This results from a lack of intimacy with the Lord. Many of us may recall the story of the football player who caught a pass and ran all the way to the opponents goal line! Can you just picture that? Without a proper perspective, God's goal line for our lives becomes blurred. Our focus on the patterns (the right plays) and our timing is off, causing us to run full steam in the opposite direction! This fellow probably was well meaning, but seriously misguided.

God's Favorite Number

How many of us have a favorite number, or maybe several of them? Why do we have them? Do they mean anything to us? Is there any real significance to them? Often, they trigger a reference to people, places and things. They can have a focal point in time, and effect our lives in different ways. God has a favorite number as well. His number is tied to His perspective/focus. It has eternity written in it. His favorite number is three. Here are some examples:

Father	Son	Holy Spirit
Spirit	Soul	Body
Most Holy Place	Holy Place	Outer Court
Feast of Tabernacles	Feast of Pentecost	Feast of Passover
Tablets (testimony)	Golden Pot of Manna	Aaron's Rod that Budded
100-Fold	60-fold	30-fold
Son	Youth	Child
Baptism in Fire	Baptism in the Holy Spirit	Baptism in Water

Not only is God's perspective and focus seen, but also His very nature is revealed. He presents Himself in three-fold patterns and practical types, from the Bible and life itself. Look through your Bible and notice how many things God expresses in threes! Three may be an odd number to the world's mind, but to us who believe, it is a beautiful and wonderful number.

My Father's House

I will be interpreting God's perspective/focus from a spiritual viewpoint. This is not to say there won't be any literal manifestations in God's economy of things. As the apostle Paul wrote:

> But as it is written, eye hath not seen, nor ear heard, neither have entered into the heart of man, the things which God hath prepared for them that love Him. But God hath revealed them unto us by His Spirit: for the Spirit searcheth all things, yea, the deep things of God. For what man knoweth the things of a man, save the spirit of man which is in him? Even so the things of God knoweth no man, but the Spirit of God. (I Corinthians 2:9-11)

Since God is spirit and the Father of spirits (Hebrews 12:9), it makes divine sense that the things that we receive from God are from the realm of the spirit.

> God is a spirit: and they that worship Him must worship Him in spirit and in truth. (John 4:24)
> Now we have received, not the spirit of the world, but the spirit which is of God; that we might know the things that are freely given to

us of God. Which things also we speak, not in the words which man's wisdom teacheth, but which the Holy Ghost teacheth; comparing spiritual things with spiritual. (I Corinthians 2:12-13)

We need to submit our mansion mentality to God's view of things—His perspective. Therefore, let's consider some familiar scripture passages:

> In my Father's house are many dwelling places; if it were not so, I would have told you; for I go to prepare a place for you. And if I go and prepare a place for you, I will come again, and receive you to Myself; that where I am, there you may be also. (John 14:2-3 NASB)
>
> In that day you shall know that I am in My Father, and you in Me, and I in you...Jesus answered and said to him, "If anyone loves Me, he will keep My word; and My Father will love him, and We will come to him, and make Our abode with him. (John 14:20, 23 NASB)
>
> In whom the whole building, being fitted together is growing into a holy temple in the Lord; in whom you also are being built together into a dwelling of God in the Spirit. (Ephesians 2:21-22 NASB).
>
> Know ye not that ye are the temple of God and that the Spirit of God dwelleth in you? (I Corinthians 3:16)
>
> What? Know you not that your body is the temple of the Holy Ghost which is in you, which ye have of God, and ye are not your own? (I Corinthians 6:19)
>
> And what agreement hath the temple of God with idols? For ye are the temple of the living God: as God has said, I will dwell in

them, and walk in them; and I will be their God, and they shall be My people. (II Corinthians 6:16)

A minister in the sanctuary, and in the true tabernacle, which the Lord pitched and not man. (Hebrews 8:2 NASB)

From this mini topical study, we are confronted with God's perspective (Colossians 1:27; I John 4:17b), causing us to take on a fresh focus in our lives. The Lord is showing us that He lives and dwells in you and me—"tabernacles not made with hands."

After reading in the book of Hebrews chapter nine, we see how the patterns of the tabernacle of Moses are for us now, who are the tabernacle of God. The Bible indicates that Moses' tabernacle is the natural pattern for the spiritual reality (I Corinthians 15:46). Jesus is the pattern Son, therefore, it behooves us to reconsider the tabernacle of Moses from God's viewpoint for our lives today.

Patterns and Times

You can recount the detailed furnishings and priestly functions in the tabernacle by reviewing the books of Exodus, Leviticus, and Numbers, along with Hebrews the ninth chapter. In addition, for handy reference of pattern applications, I am providing some charts for your study and use:

CHART A - GOD'S FOCUS FOR JESUS, THE PATTERN SON

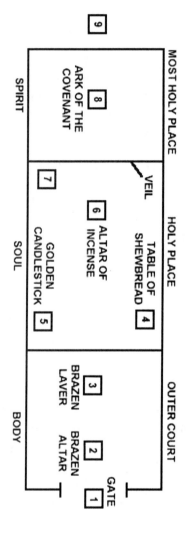

CHART A - GOD'S FOCUS FOR JESUS, THE PATTERN SON

1. Jesus is the gate or door. John 14:6.
2. Jesus is the sacrificial lamb. John 1:29; I Corinthians 5:7.
3. Jesus is our sanctifier. I Corinthians 1:30.
4. Jesus is the bread of life. John 6:48.
5. Jesus is the light of the world. John 8:12.
6. Jesus is our high priest. Hebrews 7:26.
7. Jesus' flesh is the veil. Hebrews 10:20.
8. Jesus is our King/Priest and Lord. Hebrews 7:17; Romans 14:9.
9. The alignment of the tabernacle. Heb. 8:2, 5; 9:11, 21, 23. The furniture shows the cross of Jesus.

What a marvelous picture in human form, revealing God's purposes for His people! From Savior to Son, Jesus provides a basic pattern to follow, as we journey on our trek to become Him in the earth. What is needed are some additional patterns, coupled with God's timing; in order to give us a fresh sense of where we are on our journey into God's perspective.

CHART B - GOD'S FOCUS FOR US (THE CHURCH) AS SONS

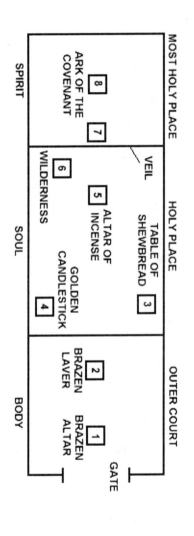

CHART B - GOD'S FOCUS FOR US (THE CHURCH) AS SONS

1. Justification by Faith
      Habakkuk 2:4;
      Romans 4
   Faith Toward God
      Hebrews 6:1
   Divine Healing in the Atonement
      I Peter 2:24
2. Water Baptism
      Matthew 28:19,20
   Sanctification
      Ephesians 5:26-27
   Washing of Regeneration
      Titus 3:5
3. Lord's Supper
      I Corinthians 11:23-30
   Divine Health/Prosperity
      III John 2
   Covenant/Community
      Acts 4:32-35;
      Ephesians 4:16
   Five-fold Ministry
      Ephesians 4:11-12
   Body Ministry
      I Corinthians 12
   Apostles' Doctrine Acts 2:42
4. Baptism in the Holy Spirit.
      Acts 1:8, 2:4, 5:32;
      Ephesians 5:18
   Fruits/Gifts of the Holy Spirit
      Galatians 5:22-23;
      I Corinthians 12:8-10
   Deliverance/Miracles
      Mark 16:17, 20
   Laying on of Hands

Hebrews 6:2
5. Spirit-filled Prayer
   John 4:23-24;
   Romans 8:26-27
   Praise and Worship
   I Corinthians 14-15
   Intercession-Priesthood of Believers
   Ephesians 6:18; 1 Peter 2:5, 9
6. Access into the Most Holy Place
   Hebrews 6:19; 10:20
7. Baptism of Fire
   Matthew 3:11;
   Hebrews 12:29
8. The Throne of God
   Revelation 3:20; 17; 21:5; 22:3-4
   Divine Life
   I John 3:2;
   Revelation 22:5
   Full Maturity
   Ephesians 4:13
   Melchisedec Priesthood
   Hebrews 6:20;
   Revelation 1:6
   Overcomers
   John 16:33;
   Romans 8:37;
   Revelation 21:7
   Foundational Ministries:
       (Apostles and Prophets)
   Ephesians 2:18, 20
   Kingdom of God
   Luke 17:21;
   I Thessalonians 2:12

To introduce our next chart, which contains a crucial element of timing, the following texts are given:

Three times in a year shall all thy males appear before the Lord thy God in the place which He shall choose; in the feast of unleavened bread, and in the feast of weeks, and in the feast of tabernacles: and they shall not appear before the Lord empty. (Deuteronomy 16:16)

Come, and let us return unto the Lord: for He hath torn, and He will heal us; He hath smitten, and He will bind us up. After two days will He revive us: In the third day He will raise us up, and we shall live in His sight. (Hosea 6:1-2)

CHART C - PATTERNS AND TIMING

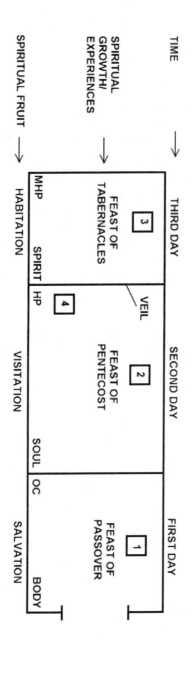

	THIRD DAY	SECOND DAY	FIRST DAY
TIME →			
SPIRITUAL GROWTH/ EXPERIENCES →	FEAST OF TABERNACLES [3]	VEIL / FEAST OF PENTECOST [2] [4]	FEAST OF PASSOVER [1]
SPIRITUAL FRUIT →	MHP HABITATION SPIRIT	HP SOUL OC VISITATION	BODY SALVATION

18

CHART C - PATTERNS AND TIMING

1. First Day

A timing focal point that we reference with II Peter 3:8 tells us that a "thousand years is as a day."

We note the first day, as the beginning of three phases of our walk into God's perspective. It is extremely important to know where we have been and why we have been there, as well as where we are going, to discern with sober judgement and understanding where we are now.

The first three focal points of our Christian walk are patterned after three feasts of the Lord which were to be celebrated perpetually (Deuteronomy 16:16).

The first focal point is the Feast of Passover. Keep in mind that as Jesus typified all of the feasts, furniture, and functions of the tabernacle, so we will be unveiled at each juncture in the tabernacle, becoming "Christ in you, the hope of glory" (Colossians 1:27).

The Feast of Passover signifies our salvation by the blood of Jesus, being applied to the door posts of our hearts. Death is traded for life as we experience a radical change in our hearts and lives. The Bible calls it the new birth. Many of us recall our salvation experience. Many of us had a violent transformation take place, wrenching us from the darkness of the evil one and changing our family status.

Salvation also gave us a new name— Christians! Jesus paid the price for you and me, that His nature might be released and seen in each of us. Hosea speaks prophetically of this experience as being "torn" and "smitten" (Hosea 6:1). God literally tore away the world's death traps from us by allowing difficult, if not tragic, circumstances to smite us as the Holy Spirit brought repentance, regeneration, and renewal into our hearts and lives. God never promised an escape theology, but a walk of victory through the circumstances (tribulations) of life.

Salvation, which literally means *a deliverance*, is a series of unveilings that begin in this outer court experience. The light of salvation, which is a deliverance from the darkness of eternal death and separation, unveils a new spirit wherein dwells righteousness. This process is declared by Paul:

> Who delivered us from so great a death, and doth deliver: and Whom we trust that He will yet deliver us. (I Corinthians 1:10)

Our spirit man was delivered (redeemed). Our soul man is being delivered (restored), and our bodies will be delivered (resurrected).

2. Second Day

We move forward to look now at the reality of the second day, as it's close is upon us. In Hosea 6:2, he spoke and said, "After two days will He revive us." This is exactly what God has accomplished through the revivals and out-pourings through the 1900's. From Azusa Street in California to Brownsville, Florida, God has demonstrated and fulfilled another feast, providing the pattern for our progress. This is the Feast of Pentecost.

The feast of Pentecost corresponds to the Holy Place in the tabernacle, along with its accompanying furniture. It signified a Spirit-filled walk with ministry attested to by manifestations of the

Holy Spirit. We now call these happenings, visitations. Hosea refers to this time period as revival. These renewals, or visitations of the life and power of God, are fresh unveilings of His life that once was, but now is. His life has been revived, brought forth, unveiled, and released.

3. Third Day

The hourglass of the tabernacle shows us there is another day, with another corresponding feast. Hosea refers to this period of time as the third day. As we approach the fading hours of day two, we come to realize that the third day from Jesus is now upon us, chronologically and spiritually. We now see a clearer view of our focal points of patterns and timing.

Hosea declares that in the third day, "He will raise us up, and we shall live in His sight" (Hosea 6:2). It is getting exciting as we look back on the first and second day feasts with their marvelous experiences and unveilings. Yet, a third day and room remains, with fresh experiences, unveilings, and a new feast as well. Our diagram depicts our fresh feast as the Feast of Tabernacles.

Tabernacles means ingathering or indwelling. The product or fruit of this feast will be that of HABITATION. This is a marked difference from the second day which was VISITATION. The anointing on the second day of Pentecost lifted, but the anointing on this third day of Tabernacles will abide.

Tabernacles will be marked by fresh emphasis from the Lord in areas like revelation, doctrine, baptism of fire, the grace of God, and the glory of God, etc. This feast, with the other two preceding ones, will graphically provide the focal pattern and timing, bringing us full-faced into the perspective, the big picture, of our God.

4. Where are we now?

As you can see on our diagram, I have placed the number 4 in front of the area of the veil into the Most Holy Place. Many of you have experienced the first two feasts and now see impending changes into a third. Transition is the verb that alludes to our place in time and guides the economy of things.

You might think nothing is happening, but I assure you things are definitely happening, and movement forward is already placed in the hearts of many in the body of Christ. Remember, we stated previously, that focus is made up of patterns over time. When we see where we have been, and get a fresh glimpse of what lies ahead, then we are able to see where we are now! Suffice it to say, if you know there is more for you in God now, then rejoice, for you are on your way!

CHAPTER TWO

THE ORDER IS CHANGING

*I*t is my belief that God's favorite number is three. It really strikes home, as we recall that Jesus was raised on the third day. Hosea prophesied that in the "third day" we will be raised up (restored) and live (Zoe'] in His sight (Hosea 6:2). As we embark on our journey into the third day of God, there are numerous changes in our becoming Him in the earth.

The old order in the first day/second day patterns are making way for the new order patterns of the third day. The Apostle Peter alludes to this unique happening. He tells us to retain what we have learned, but be established in PRESENT TRUTH (II Peter 1:12). The workings of God in us are continual, and He is systematically unveiling the old and revealing the new almost simultaneously. This work takes forward motion, and through this motion it transforms all three days into progressive patterns. This provides us with focus, showing us what the Bible calls the perfect or perfection.

> But when that which is perfect is come, then that which is in part shall be done away. (I Corinthians 13:10)
> Are you so foolish? Having begun in the Spirit, are ye now made perfect by the flesh? (Galatians 3:3)

Unfortunately, every move of God begins in the Spirit, but ends up in the flesh. You might ask, "Why is this so?" I believe the answer lies in the fact that the flesh-man always has to add his two cents worth. He tries to keep current with things God has already established and done in the past. God says, "Behold, I do a new thing." We must discern the times, seeing that God is indeed moving on. The key is that we must let God do it. We must take our hands off. We have a very good second day / third day illustration of this transition. It occurs during the days of King David as he attempts to get the Ark of God back home.

A Prophetic Glance Toward Tabernacles

And David went up, and all Israel, to Baalah, that is, to Kirjath-jearim, which belonged to Judah, to bring up thence the ark of God the Lord, that dwelleth between the cherubims, Whose name is called on it. And they carried the ark of God in a new cart out of the house of Abinadab: and Uzzah and Ahio drave the cart...And when they came unto the threshing floor of Chidon, Uzzah put forth his hand to hold the ark; for the oxen stumbled. And the anger of the Lord was kindled against Uzzah, and he smote, because he put his hand to the ark; and there he died before God. (I Chronicles 13:6-7, 9-10)

Then David said, 'None are to carry the Ark of God but the Levites: for them hath the Lord chosen to carry the ark of God, and to minister unto him forever.' And David called for Zadok and Abiathar the priests, and for the Levites, for Uriel, Asaiah, and Joel, Shemaiah, and Eliel, and Amminadab. And he said unto them, 'Ye are the chief of the fathers of the Levites: sanctify yourselves,

both ye and your brethren, that ye may
bring up the ark of the Lord God of Israel
unto the place that I have prepared for it.
For because ye did it not at the first, the
Lord our God made a breach upon us, for
that we sought Him not after the due order.'
So the priests and the Levites sanctified
themselves to bring up the ark of the Lord
God of Israel. And the children of the Levites
bare the ark of God upon their shoulders
with the staves thereon, as Moses
commanded according to the word of the
Lord. (I Chronicles 15:2, 11-15)

Just as Paul stressed the point to the
Galatians, regarding arriving at perfection with
man's help, David also learned this valuable
lesson in order to foreshadow our third day Feast
of Tabernacles. David fell into the trap, like we
often do, of trying to help God get the job done by
any old way. Since the ark was already in the
hands of the people of Philistia (type of flesh),
David should have been more discerning.

Sometimes we have costly lessons to put us
back on the path. This story may be somewhat
familiar to us, nevertheless, let us look at it from
a little different slant. Two key phrases we will
give our attention to are: "a new cart" (I
Chronicles 13:7), and "after the due order" (I
Chronicles 15:13). Another account of this story
is found in 1 Samuel 6, but we get God's
viewpoint of things in the book of the Chronicles.

God was developing His heart in David's heart.
As a minstrel/prophet, King David saw the King
of Glory during his times of worship to God. I
believe he saw the temple of God, you and me,
with the ark (Word of the Lord) dwelling within

us. I feel that God put this destiny in his heart by the Holy Spirit.

This new cart wasn't anything new at all. As a matter of fact, it was business-as-usual for the mind of the flesh. What was the cart like? I Chronicles 6:6-9, reveals to us that three things were involved in the process of taking the ark from the prophets of Philistia to Jerusalem:

1. A cart - consisting of two big wheels and several boards.

2. Two drivers - Uzzah and Ahio.

3. A drive force - oxen.

It is one thing for you to be in Egypt (the world) or Philistia (the flesh), but it is quite another for Egypt or Philistia to be in you! How do we know this? In the first scenario, the separation from Egypt and Philistia is based on our outward environment and surroundings, but in the second, the separation is based on our inward heart condition influenced by revelation received. For example, the Philistines who touched and carried the ark did not die (I Samuel 5). On the other hand, Uzzah touched the ark and died on the spot! The Israelites had revelation, but the Philistines did not.

> In that they show the work of the law written in their hearts, their conscience bearing witness, and their thoughts alternately accusing or else defending them. (Romans 2:15 NASB)
>
> Therefore having overlooked the times of ignorance, God is now declaring to men that all everywhere should repent. (Acts 17:30 NASB)
>
> And from everyone who has been given much shall much be required; and to whom

they entrusted much, of him will they ask all
the more. (Luke 12:48b NASB)

Since God was initiating spiritual changes, He
could not allow the old order to influence what He
was currently doing. Let's look at the new cart
from the second day order of things.

1. The cart - the word of the Lord carried and
brought forth by two "big wheels" (the pastor and
assistant pastor) with several boards (usually the
deacons or family members that run the show).

2. Two drivers - Uzzah, whose name means
"strength," and Ahio, whose name means "his
brother." So we have *the double strength of* man
leading the ark (word of the Lord).

3. Drive force - oxen (castrated bulls unable to
reproduce the life within themselves). The oxen do
what they are told to do, asking no questions.
They are driven by the strength of a man-made
cart with drivers, indicating a religious
organization. When things begin to get tough, the
male strength touches and manhandles the ark
(Word of the Lord), maneuvering it's place in the
scheme of things (I Chronicles 13:9).

Now God steps in with some awesome lessons
and insights. Even though David was used to
establish the second day (revival), placing the ark
in the temple foreshadowed the Feast of
Tabernacles for us. This transition was marked
by major change. Remember that there is another
key phrase - "after the due order" (I Chronicles
15:13). God now quickens David in the fifteenth
chapter of 1 Chronicles as to what the due order
is all about. The scriptures reveal that the Levites,
lead by the chief priest, are to carry the ark and
minister before the Lord. For our example and
instruction (I Corinthians 10:11 NIV), Paul gives

us the current pattern for this transition into the third day ministry. We find it in Ephesians 4:11-12:

> And He gave some as apostles, and some as prophets, and some as evangelists, and some as pastors and teachers, for the equipping of the saints for the work of service, to the building up of the body of Christ. (NASB)

The order is changing: no longer an Aaronic priesthood, but the Melchisedec priesthood (Hebrews 7); no longer a professional clergy with endless religious rules and regulations, but one of the five-fold ministry; no longer the Levitical tribe out of Israel to minister before the Lord, but now a called-out, glory-filled people chosen to bear the image of Him who rules and reigns in all the earth. These ministers are God's anointed servants to release the multi-faceted grace and glory of the Lord.

> Who also hath made us able ministers of the New Testament; not of the letter, but of the spirit: for the letter killeth, but the spirit giveth life...But we all, with open face beholding as in a glass the glory of the Lord, are changed into the same image from glory to glory, even as by the Spirit of the Lord. (II Corinthians 3:6, 18)

CHAPTER THREE

PHILISTIA - WITH PROPHETS IN THE MIDST

As the Lord takes us through the transition from the second day into the third day, we must see clearly what is being revealed. The Church has been so elated in her boasting of being delivered from Egypt, she has become blinded to the deadly reality of Philistia and the Philistines. The Apostle Paul saw this deadly reality when he wrote to the Galatians warning them about the man of flesh:

> Are you so foolish? Having begun in the Spirit, are you now made perfect by the flesh? (Galatians 3:3)

Philistia and the Philistines provide a vivid portrayal of the character of the flesh-man, or worse yet, a religious flesh-man. It is at this point that God hones in on the inward realities of the heart and soul of His Church body. The Philistines are known for their strength, size, verbal claims, outward array, and organized structures and strategies of mobilization. Unfortunately, these influences have come up through the New Testament church to the present. Two interesting examples come to mind. The first one is that of the Pharisees:

> Therefore all that they tell you, do and observe, but do not do according to their deeds; for they say things, and do not do them. And they tie up heavy loads, and lay them on men's shoulders; but they them-

selves are unwilling to move them with so much as a finger.

But they do all their deeds to be noticed by men; for they broaden their phylacteries and lengthen the tassels of their garments. And they love the place of honor at banquets, and the chief seat in the synagogues, and respectful greetings in the market places, and being called by men, Rabbi...

Woe to you, scribes and Pharisees, hypocrites, because you shut off the kingdom of heaven from men; for you do not enter in yourselves, nor do you allow those who are entering to go in.

Woe to you, scribes and Pharisees, hypocrites, because you devour widows' houses, even while for a pretense you make long prayers; therefore you shall receive greater condemnation.

Woe to you, scribes and Pharisees, hypocrites, because you travel about on sea and land to make one proselyte; and when he becomes one, you make him twice as much a son of hell as yourselves...

Woe to you, scribes and Pharisees, hypocrites! For you clean the outside of the cup and of the dish, but inside they are full of robbery and self-indulgence. You blind Pharisee, first clean the inside of the cup and the dish, so that the outside of it may become clean also.

Woe to you, scribes and Pharisees, hypocrites! For you are like white washed tombs which on the outside appear beautiful, but inside they are full of dead men's bones and all uncleanness. Even so you too outwardly appear righteous to men, but inwardly you are full of hypocrisy and lawlessness.

Woe to you, scribes and Pharisees, hypocrites! For you build the tombs of the prophets and adorn the monuments of the righteous, and say, 'If we had been living in the days of our fathers, we would not have been partners with them in shedding the blood of the prophets'. (Matthew 23:3-7, 13-15, 25-30 NASB)

The second is our dear brother Peter:

Now Peter and his companions had been overcome with sleep; but when they were fully awake, they saw His glory and the two men standing with him. And it came about, as these were parting from him, Peter said to Jesus, 'Master, it is good for us to be here; and let us make three tabernacles: one for You, and one for Moses, and one for Elijah' not realizing what he was saying. (Luke 9:32-33 NASB)

We need to ask ourselves what similarities exist between Peter and the Pharisees. Do you see any? First, they both walked in deception or a state of slumber (no clear vision). Second, both of their attitudes manifested what they wanted. Third, they liked titles and to drop names with their own. Fourth, they wanted attention and credit for participation. Fifth, and the most dangerous, they wanted their names identified with what God was doing! As born again, Spirit-filled Christians, what would you call the behavioral characteristics just described? Even worse, these attributes of the Philistines and Peter sound like much of the church world! If we are saved and filled with the Holy Spirit, then what (or who) in us would act this way? This has been a mystery that is now coming to light as God reveals it.

When everybody is about to throw in the towel, God begins to move. How? He sends a company of prophets to declare His doings. The Bible states that God will do nothing except He first will reveal it to His servants, the prophets (Amos 3:7). Notice the beautiful pattern:

> After that thou shalt come to the hill of God, where is the garrison of the Philistines: and it shall come to pass, when thou art come thither to the city, that thou shalt meet a company of prophets coming down from the high place with a psaltery, and a tabret, and a pipe, and a harp, before them; and they shall prophesy: And the Spirit of the Lord will come upon thee, and thou shalt prophesy with them, and shalt be turned into another man. (I Samuel 10:5-6)

Something awesome happens here. This is not just a little gathering with a word or two of prophecy given. What takes place is on a higher order of the Spirit of God. There is an activation and release of the Kingdom of God in a fresh dimension through a man's life. This foreshadows the establishment of a company of prophets in the body of Christ today.

Another scripture adding backbone to this thought is:

The voice of him that crieth in the wilderness, prepare ye the way of the Lord, make straight in the desert a highway for our God. (Isaiah 40:5)

Something is released and activated by the mouth of the Lord (His prophetic mantle/ company of prophets). What is it? It is the glory of the Lord. More specifically, it is the glory of His kingdom!

The new order we are entering has a fresh feast, covenant, law, and glory to be received. It will be activated by His holy apostles and prophets in these last days. This is essential for us as king/priests, since we have been called into a more excellent ministry of better things (Hebrews 8:6).

CHAPTER FOUR

SHOW US THE GLORY - WHERE IS IT?

Many people are curious about a lot of things in life. This tends to carry over into spiritual arenas as well. We are always saying to others, "Show me!" or "I want to see!" Children probably exemplify this trait best of all. Youth and frivolity tend to lean towards this thing called curiosity. This curiosity in itself can be good, or it can be quite deadly. Do you remember touching the gas stove for the first time (or two), because you were curious about those colorful elusive flames? There was a price to pay for that bold curiosity wasn't there? I believe curiosity is one of the ways that God begins to position us for further development in our Christian walk. God uses curiosity in hearts and minds of open Christians, to prepare them for fresh experiences and responsibilities in Him. Curiosity is a tool used to cause us to forge ahead into the unknown, whether good or bad.

However, with curiosity comes responsibility. Failing to respond maturely could be disastrous - even deadly. We all know that "curiosity killed the cat!" We must be responsible for our actions and not blame anyone else. You might question, "Will I get burned by the flames if I touch?" Actually, in God, the answer is yes and no. You will get consumed, but NOT burned up (destroyed). Curiosity, coupled with desire, is a tool used by the Master's hand to lead us into His perfect will. The word tells us in Revelation, the seventeenth chapter, "God hath put in their hearts to fulfill His will" (Revelation 17:17). How does He do that?

He does it using curiosity and desire - right into the things of God!

Many of you are starting to step forward not really knowing where or why, but there is a curiosity, a draw, or a desire deep down to reach out. We don't totally understand, except that we aren't comfortable anymore with our spiritual status quo. We want more of God, and we are not satisfied with church as usual. We may not be sure of all that we believe in anymore, however, we have a longing for the Lord.

When we reach out into the unknown, even in our immaturity, the word of God says that we shall be led and carried forth by another, in directions not of our previous understanding or choice (see John 21:18-19). To top it off, the Lord says that this action and yielding on our parts will bring glory to God. Yes, it will also bring death, not of the destroying kind, but the consuming kind. It is a fire that consumes everything in you and me that is not like Jesus.

Is there any good to come out of this fiery experience? Yes, I think part of the answer lies in a mystery with the word curious, the root of the word curiosity which we have been looking at. In New Testament Greek, the word for Lord is KURIOS (pronounced the same as curious). First, the curious (in the natural) and desiring child of God reaches forth into the uncharted, unknown, untested realms of God; then the hand of another (Holy Spirit) takes our hand and leads us into the wilderness. We are confronted by the fire of God and the glory of His Kingdom. The outcome will be that He becomes Kurios (Lord, now in the spiritual) in each of us (I Corinthians 15:46; I John 4:17).

Where is the glory? Many of us are being drawn by the Lord to reach out into the heavenlies for more of Him. However, to have more of Him, necessitates that there be less of us. The scripture states that an increase of Him will require a decrease of me (John 3:30). This journey will require letting go of the controls, allowing God to lead us into His realms of glory and grace by His Spirit, even though the journey may be unnerving.

You might ask, "How does God start to prepare me for this journey of transition and change, leading me into the realm of His glory?" He is doing it in some unique ways. Just prior to the onset of the curious stage, several unnerving things begin to manifest. First, we don't sense His presence much anymore. Secondly, we feel dry spiritually. Thirdly, we are not sure what we believe anymore. We are just at the point of throwing up our hands and saying, "Where is God, and what is my purpose now?"

If you find yourself like this, then the Lord may be planning an adventure of a lifetime for you. This adventure is one that we think should be reserved for people like Davy Crockett, Daniel Boone, Sergeant Preston of the Yukon, or John Wayne. But this WILDERNESS adventure is divinely planned for the sons of God, as it was for the Son of God.

Show us the glory! Where is it?

> It is the glory of God to conceal a thing: but the honor of kings is to search out a matter. (Proverbs 25:2)

UNIT II
THE WILDERNESS ADVENTURE

Chapter Five

The Prerequisite - To The Glory

Most of us want excitement and fun, but not with difficulty added to it. In other words, we don't want it if it is costly or demanding. Let us just pay the fare and watch the adventure from a distance. But this adventure is totally different.

We are the main characters being acted upon as we venture into the wilderness of God. Furthermore, we didn't pay the fare, He did! Jesus paid the fare with His life. The word indicates that He suffered through His wilderness adventure so that we, "many sons," might come unto glory (Hebrews 2:10).

The ending of our journey may appear to be sad, but to the contrary, it is rather glorious. The Bible tells us that life comes from death. It also declares to us that if we want to live then we must die, not physically or spiritually, but soulishly. The realm of the soul is where the flesh-man resides (or tries to) in each of us. Jesus battled with this also in the garden. He faced the man-of-flesh in His own life, sweating great drops of blood, and briefly yielded to the immense pressure to do His own thing! But, praise God He didn't follow through. Instead, He put the old man to death; obeyed the Father; triumphed over death; and became the Father's will in the earth. We are given this pattern in the scriptures:

And they overcame him by the blood of the lamb, and by the word of their testimony; and they loved not their lives unto the death. (Revelation 12:11)

Because as He is, so are we in this world. (I John 4:17b)

It is interesting to note that the word for "life" in Revelation 12:11 is *psuche*, meaning soul life, which is where the flesh-man must be put to death. This brings up an important point here. I believe we have had an inaccurate understanding about the Kingdom and violence that warrants another look:

And from the days of John the Baptist until now the kingdom of Heaven suffereth violence, and the violent take it by force. (Matthew 11:12)

The law and the prophets were until John: since that time the Kingdom of God is preached and every man presseth into it. (Luke 16:16)

We need to see fresh truth, the Kingdom of God is apprehended and received in us through death. We are not talking about spirit salvation, but soul salvation where the old man is put away from our lives and the Kingdom of God is received and released. Remember, being in the Kingdom does NOT mean the Kingdom is in you. Ishmael (type of flesh-man) had to be put out before Isaac (type of Kingdom man) could be weaned and released.

It was imperative that Jesus temporarily yield to and experience the man of flesh in the garden (wilderness). Why? He had to become flesh as well as sin to bring complete deliverance in both realms. He had to experience death to the man of flesh for us. Had He not done so, the flesh-man would have gained residence causing Jesus to maneuver God to an alternate plan ("PLAN B"), to accomplish redemption in the earth. Had Jesus proceeded (thank God He didn't), He would have taken the mark of 6-6-6 (66 BOOKS OF THE BIBLE/WORD; 6, number for flesh-man), DOING THE WORD OF GOD MAN'S WAY.

To increase in God, there must be a corresponding decrease. Flesh and spirit cannot co-habit together. Even in the book of Revelation we are told in the third chapter:

> I know thy works, that thou art neither cold nor hot: I would thou wert cold or hot. So then because thou art lukewarm, and neither cold nor hot, I will spue thee out of My mouth. (Revelation 3:15-16)

God obviously hates mixture. It is most deadly. It appears to correspond to religious people. The Apostle Paul gave strong warnings to Timothy concerning such people's inward makeup:

> Having a form of godliness, but denying the power thereof: from such turn away...Ever learning, and never able to come to the knowledge of the truth. (II Timothy 3:5, 7)

These individuals aren't really what they appear. They may say all the right things with their mouths, but their hearts are far removed.

Marks of Mixture

How do we know if we have mixture in us or not? Here is a list of practical questions to ask ourselves regarding this issue:

1. Is your ministry focused more on you than on the God in you?
2. Is your motive more in the receive mode than in the give mode?
3. You have no desire to support any other ministries that are truly productive?
4. Do you resist letting God trash your theology as needed?
5. Do you want your ministry more than you want Him?
6. Do you just do what you want to do, instead of what is needed?
7. Do you find that when you don't want to help, you claim that you just don't "feel led"?
8. Do you tell people what to do, rather than lead by example?
9. Are you willing to leave your family to fulfill your ministry calling?
10. Do you change churches frequently looking for recognition, authority, or support?
11. Do you just hear what you want to hear from personal prophecies?
12. Are you resistant to being involved in personal, intimate relationships with some accountability?

If you answered yes to one or more of these questions then it is my sincere prayer that God will call you into the wilderness adventure that you might be changed, preparing you to receive the glory of the Lord.

Are there signals to indicate whether we might already be in the wilderness? Here are some to consider:

1. A sense of spiritual isolation while being around other Christians regularly.
2. You don't feel His closeness, but know He is there.
3. You don't seem to have/sense spiritual purpose anymore.
4. You're not sure at times what you believe anymore.
5. You're not fulfilled with church as usual.
6. You feel dry spiritually and don't really know why.
7. You have a real sense that there is more in God.

The wilderness is the best place to be at this very season of time. It is a temporary place which results in a radical change of focus, bringing perspective (God's big picture) into clarity and understanding. Remember, God wants us to be like the men of Issachar, knowing the times and what to do (I Chronicles 12:32). Take a quick peek back to Chart B in the first section, noticing where the wilderness is positioned. It is right in front of the veil to the Most Holy Place. It is the dawning of a new day. It is the third day ministry of Jesus to the Church that is wooing us on (actually up). Jesus is saying, "come up hither," by the Spirit that He might be enthroned in each of us; in order that the Kingdom of God might be established in the earth (you).

The Bible declares a woe to those who are at ease in Zion. God is moving on and they don't even notice that the cloud has moved. God help us! Lord, don't let us be like Samson, who compromised his anointing, and didn't realize that it had gone (Judges 16:20).

Lord-Draw Us

If we want the glory then we must go through the wilderness adventure. Does it look exciting? Not exactly. Is it distressing? At times. Do we have control of things? Not really. Simply put, either we yield to God's leading and be changed, or resist and be crushed by the Master Potter.

As we reflect upon different characters in the Bible, we notice something very remarkable. Many of them had wilderness adventures with God, bringing enlargement, power, and glory into their lives:

> Noah in the ark.
> Moses on the mount (Sinai).
> Abraham on the mount (Moriah).
> Joseph in the Pharaoh's prison house.
> David in the cave of Addulum.
> Jesus in the wilderness/in Gethsemane.
> Paul in the desert.
> John on the Isle of Patmos.

We are learning that enlargement comes through wilderness times with God. David declared this reality to us in the book of Psalms, when he said, "Lord, you have enlarged me in my distress (wilderness)" (Psalm 4:4). To summarize:

1. God is calling me on - more of Him and less of me.
2. Enlargement of Him in me means a season of wilderness adventure.
3. The wilderness contains preparation for the glory of God to be released in me.

CHAPTER SIX

THE SECRET GARDEN

*C*an you remember when you were young, having your little secret place to go to? It was probably somewhere out in the woods (wilderness). It was your little, wonderful, almost mystical hideout away from all the world. It was where your heart was open to express your innermost dreams, desires, and feelings about things of life and the world around you. You only shared it with those who you were intimate with. It was special. There was a bonding of soul and spirit that took place, a oneness, between you and your best friend, or the one you were in love with. It was a place that you went to often, and it would remain special, possibly a place of endearment, for the rest of your life.

It is for this very reason that the wilderness is a requirement to go on into the fullness of God. Only in the wilderness is found the SECRET GARDEN. This does not mean that there is no significant communication or experience with God in the busy, hustle-bustle streams of life that most of us find ourselves in. No, as a matter-of-fact, much of our Christian experience has been one in full public view and full of shared expression with our brothers and sisters in Christ. This probably has been coupled with a good basic diet of prayer and Bible study. However, this typical Christianity-as-usual experience is NOT what we are being led into by the Lord. This is a special place He has created, and therefore has special purpose. Jesus himself went and prepared a "secret place" for us, so we could enter at His leading. It is going to be very special. The Bible gives us a preview of this special occurrence, as we view it from a spiritual vantage point:

> In my Father's house are many dwelling places; if it were not so, I would have told you; for I go to prepare a place for you. And if I go and prepare a place for you, I will come again, and receive you to Myself; that where I am, there you may be also. (John 14:2-3 NASB)

Jesus went into the wilderness, and into a garden, prior to culmination on the cross. In the wilderness and the garden, Jesus found himself in a place of:

- spiritual aloneness
- temporary blur of purpose
- heavy dealings from God
- temptation from Satan
- testing from the "mystery man"

Jesus first went through the ultimate wilderness adventure to prepare a secret garden for us to come and receive the glory of God as He had also received. Jesus tells us this in the gospel of John, "And the glory which Thou gavest Me I have given them" (John 17:22). This is not all. Not only did He prepare the garden, HE BECAME IT!

Let's go back to the beginning and look at the book of Genesis.

> Therefore the Lord God sent him [Adam] forth from the garden of Eden, to till the ground from whence he was taken. So He drove out the man; and He placed at the east of the garden of Eden Cherubims, and a

flaming sword which turned every way, to keep the way of the tree of life. (Genesis 3:23-24)

Unfortunately, this picture is a rather sad one. We find Adam running away from the garden, not to return. It dispels the thought that we always run into our secret gardens. This occasion was different for Adam. Due to disobedience to God, Adam lost his sweet fellowship in the garden, requiring him to leave its wonders. The first Adam left the garden, as sin found a home where the divine nature was abating. Another nature moved in to substitute in its place. Jesus, the second Adam, patterned the way through obedience so that we might come into the secret garden and experience its life-changing wonders.

Jesus is in the midst of the garden, because He is the tree of life. He is the Life! Surrounding Him is a flaming sword which moves in such a powerful and defining way that no one enters and lives. So, who would want to walk into that? All who are called to partake of His glory. It appears painful. Often times it is a traumatic gut-wrenching experience.

We all thought at salvation that we had all there was of God. Then at the baptism of the Holy Ghost, we knew this wasn't true! Surprise! There is much more. Well, what is it? It is located in the wilderness of God, in the secret garden. It is the glory of God.

This experience for us will be somewhat similar to the one Moses had, yet distinctly different. God called Moses to the secret place (in the mountain) to receive the revelation of God, and see the glory of God pass by. Moses had to cover, or veil, his face to experience the fullness of

God. As the Lord draws many of us into the secret garden, we also see the burning bush of God. We realize that it is the tree of life - Jesus and all His glory. Consumed by fire yet not destroyed, the sword (His voice) speaks out of the midst. We didn't choose the wilderness adventure, but God chose it for us because He loves us.

The wilderness dealings of God require a prophetic voice crying out to God's people. A prophetic mantle is being released in these days to do just that. Its purpose is to give sight to the blind.

CHAPTER SEVEN

THE VEIL

Moses had a veil over his face to conceal the glory of God. Many of us today have a veil over our faces, constituting a condition that the scripture calls blindness. "This does not describe me or my church," you say. "Gee, we have one of the fastest growing churches in town; programs from the cradle to the grave; a beautiful choir and orchestra; and a sweet little pastor. Everything is administrated to a T, and runs like clockwork." Your time may have run out. Look at the Word of the Lord to the Laodicea Christian Center, a type of the present day, Spirit-filled church found in the third chapter of the book of Revelation:

> Because thou sayest, I am rich, and increased with goods, and have need of nothing; and knowest not that thou art wretched, and miserable, and poor, and blind, and naked: I counsel thee to buy of Me gold tried in the fire, that thou mayest be rich; and white raiment, that thou mayest be clothed, and that the shame of thy nakedness do not appear; and anoint thine eyes with eye-salve, that thou mayest see. (Revelation 3:17-18)

The similarities are amazing aren't they? The word used to describe a part of their condition from verse 17 is BLIND (or veiled). How can this happen? It is usually slow and subtle. It doesn't become obvious until the Lord removes the veil and reveals Himself. Otherwise, spiritual darkness would remain our portion. The scariest part is the religiously blind don't know they are blind. I am reminded of Samson in the Old Testament. When he continued to give himself to serve the creature (woman) instead of God, the scripture says of Samson that he knew not that the anointing had left him. This is why the prophetic call is given, "WAKE UP!" Paul gives us some clues into this mysterious process in the book of Romans:

> Because that, when they knew God, they glorified Him not as God, neither were thankful; but became vain in their imaginations, and their foolish heart was darkened. Professing themselves to be wise, they became fools, and changed the glory of the incorruptible God into an image made like to corruptible man, and to birds, and four-footed beasts, and creeping things. Wherefore God also gave them up to uncleanness through the lusts of their own hearts, to dishonor their own bodies between themselves. (Romans 1:21-24)

I believe this text gives some insight into what the Bible refers to as the "mystery of iniquity" (II Thessalonians 2:7). When our eyes wander away from Jesus - something takes place - the eyes of our heart become darkened or VEILED so that everything becomes blurred (a mixture). We see everything from a view that is not from God. Our perception of things is now mainly self-oriented and self-focused. The Lord warned the mature Ephesian church about this deadly posture. He said "Thou hast left thy first love" (Revelation 2:4). So how can this happen to us? Simply put, our doing becomes greater than our being. Our attention turns to the ministry of the Lord, instead of the Lord of the ministry. A supernatural exchange takes place. In the book of James, this subtle, deadly change is alluded to:

> He is like unto a man beholding his natural face in a glass: For he beholdeth himself, and goeth his way, and straightway forgetteth what manner of man he was. (Jas.1:23-24)

Something wonderfully awesome takes place as we continually gaze into the Word. We are actually changed from faith to faith and glory to glory. James gives us a revelation, with a corresponding warning:

1. James reveals that gazing into the Word causes us to be a 'certain manner of man'.
2. When we leave our posture of continuing to gaze into the Word, we forget (become blurred or veiled) from what manner we are.
3. The Apostle Paul reveals that when we leave our intimate posture of giving Him glory and thanks in all things, there is a change of image-from that of God to that liken to another man. He also states that the glory changes since the image changed.
4. James affirms that leaving our gaze of Him causes us to forget (be blinded/veiled) what glory was upon us.

The mystery of iniquity rephrased in modern terminology might say something like this: "the hidden (one) that does his own thing." So when we don't stay before the face of the Lord our image is changed from His image into another

image that is NOT the Lord! Who is this mystery
man?

CHAPTER EIGHT

THE MYSTERY MAN

*T*his mystery man is who the Lord wants to deal with once and for all. The Bible reveals that he is already at work in the hearts of each person who is not experientially walking in the lordship and kingship of Jesus Christ. The mystery man is declared by the Bible to be an enemy of God. It is the flesh-man - the carnal mind (Romans 8:7). He is a religious person, empowered by a spirit of anti-Christ (another-substitute for Christ). He is an imposter. He is the tare not the wheat. He has a form (image) of godliness but denies the power of it. He takes all the credit and glory for what he has accomplished. He promotes himself, and his trinity is Me, My, and Mine.

I believe many of us have walked in his image in ignorance - believing that if anything is accomplished in God, we must do it. The flesh-man is in the church as well as in the world, but he is getting ready to be exposed and dealt with permanently, on an experiential level. The mystery man of iniquity (or lawlessness) will restrain until he be taken out of the way (II Thessalonians 2:7 NIV). He will be dealt with according to verse 8, which is strikingly similar to what is in the middle of the secret garden. Jesus told us that the veil was represented by his flesh. He too had to go to the secret garden of Gethsemane to experience a spiritual unveiling, in order to be and do the Father's will.

What does the man of flesh and the mystery of iniquity actually restrain? I believe the answer lies in another mystery, the mystery of godliness (I Tim.3:16). This sacred secret reveals the revelation of Christ in you, the hope of glory! The man of flesh, represented by the veil, must be torn away and consumed. This will reveal the glory of God in each one of us as the Christ in the earth, to the glory of the Father.

Our salvation is stated to be experientially progressive in II Corinthians 1:10. "Who delivered us from so great a death, and doth deliver: in whom we trust that He will yet deliver us."

This consuming death of the old man in the soul realm comes into particular focus here. In order for our spirit man (already delivered) to come into union with our soul (being delivered), then the veil must be rent and the old man, i.e. flesh nature, carnal mind, must be destroyed. This is the primary purpose for the wilderness. God said he would have no other gods before His face (literally)! So the wilderness adventure into the secret garden is a must for all whom our Lord would call. With His sword and consuming fire, we will be changed into the self-same image, even by the Spirit of the Lord!

**UNIT III
THE UNVEILING...**

CHAPTER NINE

SPIRITUAL BLINDNESS

*B*lindness (the inability to see clearly or to see at all), has similar characteristics in both the natural and spiritual realms. Some of these characteristics are:

- You can't see where you have been.
- You can't see where you are.
- You can't see where you are going.
- You can't see the truth (reality).
- You judge things on what you feel.
- You want to keep things in the same old places.
- You are led by a dog (beast nature).

I believe total blindness is better than blurred vision (legally blind). The Lord inferred this Himself in the book of Revelation, the third chapter:

> So then because thou art lukewarm, and neither cold nor hot, I will spue thee out of My mouth. (Revelation 3:16)

What does lukewarm mean? It is a MIXTURE of both hot and cold. It is a blur, a double vision; it is seeing from two perspectives or natures: God's and the Devil's. We call it the flesh nature, beast nature, or the carnal mind. In another text, James tells us that a double-minded (or double-natured) man is unstable (can't see where he is going) in all his ways (James 1:8). James then states that this man shall not receive anything from the Lord. Why is this? Isn't this kind of harsh? First of all we must remember that God has called us to be people of faith. Secondly, we must remember that we referred to the blind man as a MIXTURE? Look with me again at what the Word of God says about true faith:

> For unto us was the gospel preached, as well as unto them: but the word preached did not profit them, not being mixed with faith in them that heard it. (Hebrews 4:2)

A single, clear eye (nature) sees the word of the Lord in faith and acts in obedience to the will of the Lord. These people walk in and demonstrate the divine nature in their lives. However, a blurred, double vision (nature), sees the word of the Lord in unbelief and acts in disobedience to the will of the Lord. These people walk in and demonstrate the flesh or beast nature. What does the future hold for the latter? It does not hold much without the wooing of the Lord. Look at what the writer to the Hebrews concludes about this group of people: "So we see that they could not enter in because of unbelief" (Hebrews 3:19).

Wow, that is a heavy statement! Let's put this into perspective according to what God is saying in these last days. Exactly what is it that we cannot enter into? Some of you peeked further into Hebrews 4 - seeing a REST. This is partially correct, however, it is only one characteristic and not the full scope of what is to be entered into. Occupying its position just past the veil, for those who have their veil (flesh nature) rent once and for all, is the Most Holy Place. This is signified by the feast of Tabernacles, bringing us into UNION with the Lord. We become one in Him, as well as within ourselves (spirit and soul). Please refer back to the charts at the beginning of the book, to picture this more clearly.

Remember this MIXTURE (flesh nature) is religious, but not truly spiritual. He is an imposter. Let's look at one very good example from the Bible: Lot, whose name literally means VEIL. Wow! Let's see how this nature plays out. Go to the book of Genesis, the twelfth and thirteenth chapters, and read the scenario, pointing out the particulars including the following:

1. Abram was told specifically to leave his kindred behind to follow the Lord (12:1).
2. Abram departed but took Lot (nephew) with him (12:4).
3. With Lot being included, Abram could only go in circles endeavoring to follow God (13:3).
4. The flesh nature (Lot) always has great ambitions, and always rises up against the spirit (13:5-7).
5. When opportunity is given, the flesh nature always chooses the bent towards flesh and sin (13:11-12).
6. When the flesh (Lot) has been removed, direction and promise is released (13:14-16).

Looking into the sixth characteristic briefly, we stated that the blind want nothing changed, but desire to keep everything in the same place! A good scripture highlighting this sad posture is "No man also having drunk old wine straightway desires new: for he saith, 'the old is better'" (Luke 5:39).

Jesus tells us emphatically that new wine can only be put into new wine bottles (Luke 5:37-38). Why? The old is set in its ways and doesn't want change. A spiritually blind person wants church-as-usual, with everything in the exact same place and fashion. Don't introduce any new spiritual experiences or fresh revelation, because that is not what they are used to and comfortable with.

God help us to cry out for the prophetic eye salve the Lord offers in the book of Revelation 3:18. Interestingly enough, perfect eyesight was a part of the requirements for ministry as a Levitical priest (Leviticus 21:18). You couldn't be blind and be a part of the ministry.

I wonder how many blind ministers we have in our churches today? The old order of Eli has become blurred and blind. We must have a new order - a Samuel company of prophets bringing prophetic reformation and eye-salve to the people of God that we may see what God is saying and doing in these last days.

CHAPTER TEN

VEILED FACES IN THE BIBLE

*T*here are a number of familiar faces in the Bible having a veil over their eyes. I am selecting five particular individuals to look at: Samson, Paul, Balaam, Mary at the tomb, and the Two Men on the Road to Emmaus.

Samson

Samson was called out and separated from birth, like many of us. Like Samson, we have committed our lives to the Lord. However, Samson had a major problem in his life. It was lust for a woman. Most of us are very acquainted with his life-story found in the book of Judges, the thirteenth through the sixteenth chapters. Here are some important parallel points to ponder:

1. Many of us strongly desire to be an intimate part of the church (woman) life and ministry.
2. We have been willing to share our visions, callings, and "sacred secrets" with her.
3. Our visions were taken, anointings compromised, and we were required to serve the church (woman's) system.
4. By God's mercy, some of us were able to escape the system and bare fruit in the end.

What are some painful lessons that we can learn from this story in type?

1. Our eyes must be focused on God first and foremost.

2. We must desire to please Him and not the church system or everyone in it.
3. We must never use the church to flaunt or promote our giftings.

Samson's need for self-gratification caused his blindness to the system. It brought required performance and ultimate death. To avoid the Samson syndrome, each of us must search our hearts and ask the question: "Have I, or do I, compromised my anointings just for a chance to be used, fit in, and/or be loved and wanted?"

Paul

Paul is an interesting, but scary, case of a zealot for God gone amuck. He was of Jewish stock, raised in the law, and a Pharisee (Philippians 3:6). He was zealous for God, blameless, and with impeccable doctrine. However, one thing was drastically wrong: Paul abhorred Christians because of their walk (called The Way.) Paul was a legalist in every sense of the word. As a matter of fact, he would harm or kill to prove his points. Paul took great pride in bringing pain to those of unlike beliefs.

Paul's veil of religious legalism went deeper than just harming believers. There was an underlying element that perhaps Paul didn't know, but the spirit of anti-Christ motivating him did. We find a clue into this development of his blindness in the book of Acts:

And when the blood of thy martyr Stephen was shed, I also was standing by, and consenting unto his death, and kept the raiment of them that slew him. (Acts 22:20)

Who or what was Paul really killing? I don't believe that it was Stephen. I believe it was the revelation of the Christ within him that Paul wanted to destroy! Consider this, "What does the enemy ultimately want to steal, kill, and destroy?" Is it you? NO! It is the revelation of the Christ within you!

The religious man of the flesh loves doctrine and a good, traditional exposition. What he doesn't like is a fresh move of God filled with love, revelation knowledge, and signs and wonders. His veil wants to kill others that have a different walk than his.

We must ask ourselves these questions:
1. Are we being pressed or molded to believe, perform, or minister a certain way?
2. Have I, or do I, press others to believe, flow, or minister a certain way?

Balaam

The story of Balaam carries a clear, strong warning to those in prophetic ministry. We are not going to belabor the whole story, but you can follow along in the book of Numbers, chapters 22-24. Here are some important points to consider:

1. Balaam had a genuine proven prophetic ministry.
2. He loved God and obeyed His directives.
3. His old man of flesh was not dealt with.
4. It manifested in two main areas: promotion and material gain.
5. When tempted, Balaam yielded, thereby becoming veiled.
6. He couldn't see clearly by the Spirit any longer.

7. Disobedience in the flesh caused the anointing to lift, and a counterfeit to replace the inspiration.

The prophetic ministry must be free in the Spirit to obey and follow God's leading, regardless of financial and promotional considerations. This is not to say that those who move and minister prophetically cannot be rewarded or given provision. The Bible clearly indicates that those who regularly administer the Word should also be provided for by those who receive the ministry of the Word (I Corinthians 9:13-14).

The veil, represented by the flesh-man, has at its center a system of lusts including: the lust of the eyes, the lust of the flesh, and the pride of life. This is also true in the religious area. What is so sad is that the world's ways (lust) have permeated the church "while she yet slept." Therefore she has become veiled, exhibiting a mixture of the wheat/tare nature in many of her sons and daughters.

A primary directive for the current restoration of the prophetic office is to reveal and expose this enemy of God (Romans 8:7). His revealing will be his undoing. This will take place, as we SEE in the secret garden of the wilderness (note II Thessalonians 2:8). It is imperative that the prophetic mantle not give way to promotionalism, hype, prophetic manipulation of any sort, or greed.

Greed is primarily manifested through merchandising the anointing in the house of God. We all must answer to God, giving an account of the motives and intents of our hearts concerning the market place inside the temple of the Lord.

Here is where Balaam bit the dust. His veil was revealed in the form of greed. It manifested in his desire for prophetic fame and financial gain. After temptation, he was willing to prophesy against God's people in order to fulfill the lust of his heart. You can see this clearly by what he says in Numbers:

> And Balaam answered and said unto the servants of Balak, "If Balak would give me his house full of silver and gold, I cannot go beyond the word of the Lord my God, to do less or more. Now therefore, I pray you, tarry ye also here this night, that I may know what the Lord will say unto me more." (Numbers 22:18-19)

Here we see mixture in full manifestation. Part of Balaam's heart wants to obey and follow God, while the other part wants promotion, honor and wealth. As the story continues, God Himself, stands against him in the way. Probably the most ludicrous and saddest commentary is what transpired next. The angel of the Lord stood in Balaam's way. Balaam, the man of God, didn't see him. Balaam's donkey, representing the flesh nature did see him. The real miracle of God was that the donkey yielded and spoke. The flesh nature will speak, but rarely yields to the will of God. Perhaps it would have been better for Balaam, if he had been killed by the angel of the Lord, rather than to turn into a soothsayer against God's people (Joshua 13:22).

We must ask ourselves this question: "Have I ministered, or do I minister or participate in activities having underlying motives for money and promotion, either personally or in the corporate structure/system?"

Mary at the Tomb

The small, but profound account of Mary at the tomb, provides another look at the veil. We find the storyline recorded in John 20:14-16.

> And when she had thus said, she turned herself back, and saw Jesus standing and knew not that it was Jesus. Jesus saith unto her, "Woman, why weepest thou? Whom seekest thou?" She, supposing him to be the gardener, saith unto him, "Sir, if Thou have borne Him hence, tell me where Thou hast laid Him, and I will take Him away." Jesus saith unto her, "Mary." She turned herself, and saith unto Him, "Rabboni" which is to say, Master.

We want to focus on verse 14 and 15. Let's consider these points from both natural and spiritual perspectives:
1. Mary was looking for Jesus.
2. She had a burden to minister to Him.
3. She looked at Jesus in her midst.
4. She thought He was the gardener.
5. She sought permission and approval to minister to Jesus.
6. The man, Jesus, spoke to her intimately calling her Maria (Mary).
7. Immediately she knew that it was Jesus.
8. She responded with, "Master."

I believe we have some unique revelation in this short scene. We must remember that Mary Magdalene was intimately acquainted with Jesus and knew Him well (note: John 19:25). Now in this setting, she looks right at Him and sees the gardener. The gardener, translated from the original language, means the overseer of all the grounds and workers. She saw someone in final authority to ask for permission/approval to minister the burden of her heart. What was her blindness - her veil? Her veil was the approval of man.

Approval from man can prevent us from seeing God, missing Him all together. Our intimacy with Jesus must not be compromised by the dictates of man. Are you suggesting that we shouldn't be submissive to leadership? What I am suggesting is that which the scripture affirms in the book of Acts, Chapter 5. Peter states, "We are to obey God rather than man" (5:29). God has called us to seek Him first, then in meekness we become accountable to those who God places in authority, to perfect us in love. This is not control and bondage, but release and freedom.

Godly authority and submission brings accountability, protection, and freedom to be and do all God has destined for us. In this posture, WE SEE JESUS! Outside of this posture we see mere men, having a veil over our faces, the veil being the traditions of men. Obedience to God doesn't replace accountability to leadership. It defines and gives clarity to the divine order of government in the Kingdom of God. Yielding to the controls of religious men will bring a veil. This veil replaces the vision of the Christ in all of His glory, manifesting through each of us.

We must ask ourselves this question, "Does most everything we have a vision for require double and triple approvals?"

Two Men on the Road to Emmaus

The incident concerning the two men on the road to Emmaus is found in Luke 24:13-35. Some interesting observations to consider are:

1. Their eyes were "holden" (verse 16), which means restrained.
2. They didn't know Jesus, even when He talked with them.
3. They complained about things not happening in the order that they were supposed to.
4. They were accustomed to the control and manipulation of the religious rulers of Israel.

Intimacy of ministry produced revelation and deliverance.

This story shows the dangerous reality of predetermined agendas and inflexible programs. This is what the two disciples were personally familiar with. These men trusted and went along with the program instead of trusting the person of the program.

When people follow their predetermined agenda, they become frustrated, complainers, void of personal revelation, and full of unbelief. Hence, a veil of flesh restrains and holds back the knowledge of the glory of the Lord.

As Jesus ministered through intimacy by the Spirit, the disciples' eyes were opened. They SAW him for who He was, not just a name on an agenda. One point of interest, Emmaus is eight miles from Jerusalem and eight is the number of new beginnings. These two men were on the road to a new beginning in the Spirit, requiring a supernatural deliverance from the veil of religious flesh.

Only as we yield ourselves to receive and give ministry as the Spirit leads, will we SEE Jesus manifested in our midst. The question to all of us is, "Do we have opportunities and the freedom to minister to others, or do we just serve on programs and predetermined agendas with no flexibility?"

Summing up this chapter on veiled faces, there are five ingredients of blindness produced by the veil of flesh. They were all present in the church of Laodicea. These traits are:

1. Spiritual lusts
2. Legalism
3. Greed
4. Traditions of Men
5. Manipulation/Control

Let's ask ourselves this question, "Would Jesus be a committed member of the Laodicean Christian Center?" The scripture says in Hebrews 13:13:"Let us go forth therefore unto Him without the camp, bearing His reproach."

CHAPTER ELEVEN

THE UNVEILING...

*T*his is a critical, pivotal chapter in our pilgrimage dealing with the manifestation of the glory of the Lord. As we read earlier, the glory is found in the wilderness, specifically in the secret garden.

The wilderness is not a geographical place. It is a posture that the Lord brings us into. This posture is intense at times, being best described by the word DEALINGS. It is designed to release and activate in you the glory of God with its various facets. However, we can experience more than one wilderness adventure in our Christian pilgrimage. Remember, maturity into full sonship is progressive.

The prophetic mantle is now trumpeting to those who have an "ear to hear." Are these being called to another seminar, workshop, conference, or Bible study? No, they are being called to the wilderness and the dealings of God.

These dealings provide the basis for a fresh new form of deliverance which the Lord is releasing in these last days. This deliverance is viewed more as the fire of God, versus the "come out you devil" variety. Actually, it is the fiery sword of the Lord's glory being released into your life. This separates flesh and spirit, unveiling the Christ in you, the hope of glory. Isn't this what we all want, to be Him in the earth, and manifest His glory to the world?

As those in the prophetic and apostolic mantles assume their respective roles, calling forth and releasing the glory of the Lord, we will see awesome deliverance come to God's people.

This deliverance involves a joint effort; the glory of the Lord, working in tandem with the grace of God. This will bring forth His divine nature and the glory of the Kingdom of God manifesting in and through His people. The glory of the Father (fire) with the grace of the Son (sword), as postured in the garden of Eden, join together. This causes a major spiritual deliverance to be unleashed in our lives.

This unique experience we are being called into within the secret garden of God is a mystery. What we have is the struggle of the ages! We see this in a people manifesting both the mysteries of iniquity "6-6-6" and godliness "7-7-7" within their lives. In reality, this is a MIXTURE of two natures inside one heart.

James states that a "double-minded" (or doubled-souled) man is unstable in all his ways. He also affirms that in this condition of mixture, we cannot receive anything from God. The mystery of iniquity (flesh nature) is now RESTRAINING the mystery of godliness (divine nature), in order to prevent the complete release of His glory in us. The flesh nature will be divided asunder, separated from the divine nature, and consumed. This will release the Christ nature in us. "7-7-7" is symbolic of the Christ nature representing the three-fold perfection of the glory and grace of God, manifested His way through the Church.

Even Jesus had to really contend with the flesh-man. Yes, he had wilderness experiences also! These experiences released corresponding facets of God's glory through His life, in order that the divine nature of God would become visible. Jesus told the disciples on one occasion, "the one who comes (flesh-man-inspired by Satan) has

67

nothing in Me" (John 14:30). However, His walk then, as well as ours now, was to be progressive - "glory to glory." We don't receive all of it at once to be done with it. Jesus didn't either. The writer of Hebrews relates that Jesus "learned obedience through the things (dealings-wilderness) he suffered" (Hebrews 5:8). The grande finale He faced came in the garden of Gethsemane. Once, and for all, He had a final showdown with the flesh-man. This is described for us in Matthew 26:36-44. Key spiritual points are:

1. Jesus had a veil (flesh-man), desire to do God's will "another way" (verse 39).
2. Jesus, without a veil (spirit man), also stated, "God's will be done" (verse 39).
3. The flesh-man arising in Jesus, restrained the release of the glory of the Kingdom of God through three prayer meetings with God (verse 44).
4. Jesus continued in the Father's presence until the dealings of God wrought a complete deliverance in His soul.
5. His deliverance was signified by Luke's account by referring to the "great drops of blood" (Luke 22:44).
6. Jesus as the pattern Son paved the way for us, experiencing the rending of the veil (flesh-man) in His soul (Hebrews 10:20).

Experientially and progressively, Jesus received a complete deliverance in spirit, and in His soul. As many as our God shall call, will encounter this wilderness adventure in order to be a part of the end-time manifestation of the glory of God.

The Process

We now begin to look into the mysteries, or sacred secrets, of the actual processes of the wilderness adventure. The introduction begins with a bang. Actually, the word BOMB is more appropriate. What is one thing that we think about when the word wilderness or desert is mentioned? If you said 'nuclear testing' or 'atomic bombs', you are correct. What does this have to do with my perfecting? Everything, because this is what facilitates the total wilderness adventure in our lives. Please keep in mind, we are dealing with the revelation of the Kingdom of God, which gives a spiritual (eternal) view of that which is natural (temporary):

> Howbeit that was not first which is spiritual, but that which is natural: and afterward that which is spiritual. (I Corinthians 15:46)

Let's delve into some scriptures, with our spiritual eyes, to unveil this process:

> But the day of the Lord will come as a thief in the night; into which the heavens shall pass away with a great noise, and the elements shall melt with fervent heat, the earth also and the works that are therein shall be burned up...Looking for and hasting unto the coming of the day of God, wherein the heavens being on fire shall be dissolved, and the elements shall melt with fervent heat? Nevertheless we, according to His promise, look for new heavens and a new earth, wherein dwelleth righteousness. (II Peter 3:10, 12-13)

In a moment, in the twinkling of an eye, at the last trump: for the trumpet shall sound, and the dead shall be raised incorruptible, and we shall be changed. (I Corinthians 15:52)

For the word of God is quick, and powerful, and sharper than any two-edged sword, piercing even to the dividing asunder of soul and spirit, and of the joints and marrow, and is a discerner of the thoughts and intents of the heart. (Hebrews 4:12)

Within these scriptures lies the revelation of the dealings of God:

1. We are entering the "day of God" presently (II Peter 3:8, Hosea 6:2).
2. It will be hallmarked with a fresh baptism of FIRE. It is the Father's ministry, as our God is a consuming fire (Hebrews 12:29).
3. The word of the Lord, the ministry of Jesus, will join in the process.
4. The fire of God the Father, along with the Word of the Lord Jesus, will be powerfully released, as an EXPLOSION in our lives.
5. In the above verse quoted from I Corinthians, chapter 15:
   a. "In a moment" is translated from Greek to "in an Adam" with two Greek words- the first little word is translated 'in', and the second 'atom' (Strong's number 823 in the New Testament section). Even as 'atom' represents the basic structure or nature of life in the natural, 'Adam' represents the basic structure or nature of life in the natural/spiritual! We therefore subs-

titute 'atom' for 'Adam' to arrive at our next point.

   b. Our spiritual understanding is - "in the Adam."

6. From the above verse in Hebrews chapter 4, the Greek word for "sharper" is TOMOTEROS (Strong's number 5114, in the New Testament section). It's root word means sharp - as in a single cut. Strong's number 823 provides the base for number 5114.

7. The practical translation might sound like this! - "an uncut Adam experiencing a sharp single cut."

8. Spiritually enlarged - we would have something like this: - "an undivided Adam (nature) experiencing a sharp, powerful cut."

9. Therefore, when we bring the FIRE (of God) together with the SWORD (Word of the Lord), we have an explosion - called an "ADAM BOMB."

10. This "bomb" splits asunder the Adam (natures), from being a mixture of spirit-man and flesh-man - the first and second Adam.

11. This is what happens as God draws us into the fiery sword, within the secret garden of the wilderness (II Peter 3:10, Phillips translation).

12. The "fervent heat" of God's fire consumes the "elements (principles) and works" of the flesh nature (II Peter 3:10).

13. The heavens experience restoration by fire. Our heavens (spirit and soul) are being restored by fire (Ezekiel 36:26).

14. No longer a mixture, but a "heart of flesh," indicating the divine nature coupled with the Spirit of God in our hearts.

Meditate and visualize this wonderful, awesome happening, as we look further at seven areas in the dealings of God.

Sevens

God chose the number seven to indicate perfection, or full maturity. This number is significant regarding the dealings of God, because we begin to see a seven-fold process of dealings in our wilderness adventure. Remember, the dealings of God are for one main purpose: to release the glory of God in us.

When the fire of God and the sword of the Lord come together releasing the "Adam bomb," we see two things:

1. A mushroom cloud
2. Total devastation

There is an interesting prophetic type of this event in the Song of Solomon:

> Who is this that cometh out of the wilderness like pillars of smoke, perfumed with myrrh and frankincense, with all powders of the merchant? (Song of Solomon 3:6)

We see spiritually that the wilderness experience releases:

1. Pillars of smoke (i.e. the mushroom cloud)
2. Perfumed with myrrh and frankincense (anointing oil for death and also ministry).

How appropriate, that the wilderness is meant to release the glory of God. It will be seen in our lives two ways:

1. The "glory cloud," a sign that is SEEN outwardly from our lives.
2. The devastation (dealings) of God will be UNSEEN and produce the mystery of "Christ in you the hope of glory."

The glory of God will release the grace of God in seven areas of our lives. We find this listed for us in the book of Isaiah:

> The voice of him that crieth in the wilderness, "Prepare ye the way of the Lord, make straight in the desert a highway for our God." Every valley shall be exalted, and every mountain and hill shall be made low: and the crooked shall be made straight, and the rough places plain: And the glory of the Lord shall be revealed, and all flesh shall see it together: for the mouth of the Lord hath spoken it. (Isaiah 40:3-5)

Note the voice crying FROM THE WILDERNESS, preparing the foundation for the new walk, new feast, fresh revelation and anointings. This voice is the union of the prophetic and the apostolic, as they are the foundation builders (Ephesians 2:20).

In simple outline form, here are the seven points:

1. Prepare YOU the way...
2. Make straight...
3. Valley exalted...
4. Mountains/hills made low...
5. Crooked made straight...
6. Rough made plain...
7. Glory of the Lord revealed...

What a marvelous exposition: beginning with an INVITATION to the Feast of Tabernacles in point 1 and ending with MANIFESTATION in point 7, releasing the GLORY of God, Christ in you. What we see through each area is a divine DELIVERANCE, fresh and new! The glory of God and the grace of God brings a total destruction to the flesh-man in our lives as we yield to Him in the wilderness. Following is a description of what is blown up and destroyed by the "Adam bomb," then some nuggets are given, for the Lord to enlarge and apply to our lives:

1. BLOWN UP:
   - Theologies
   - Religious traditions
   - Religious system

   (See II Timothy 3:7, 5)

The wilderness is our door into the Most Holy Place, where we are to "live, move, and have our being." Since Jesus is the door, we must leave our shoes there signifying our old religious ways, etc... as indicated. There is dust (FLESH) on our feet. Jesus will use both hands (sword/fire) to consume the flesh-man, then refresh the feet (WALK) with cool waters (HOLY SPIRIT). Remember we are reading this in good old English which says, "prepare YOU the way of the Lord!"

2. BLOWN UP:
   - Your plans
   - Your goals
   - Your direction

The Bible indicates to us that "there is a way (plan, goal, or direction) that seems right, but the ends thereof are death." Why does it end this way? Because we sense (hear) the Lord's leading, then we see (envision) it according to our strength and ability (flesh-man). Therefore, we have blurred vision (blind) and we are a mixture. Remember, when we do God's will man's way, what do we have? Right, 6-6-6. Put another way, when we don't see and obey from God's viewpoint, we take Lot along. His name means VEIL. Like the prophet Habakkuk, we must SEE what He will SAY to us (Habakkuk 2:1). We must have these "two witnesses" in order to be and do of His good pleasure. The Bible plainly tells us that God created both the seeing eye and the hearing ear (Proverbs 20:12).

3. BLOWN UP:
- Despair
- Hopelessness
- Self pity

The primary reason for these conditions is the flesh-man's influence, prompting us to compete for recognition of our gift, press for promotion over others, and to simply require attention. The scripture plainly tells us that humility must come before honor. Humility is found only in the wilderness. We see this principle at work in the book of Judges:

> And the Lord was with Judah and he drave out the inhabitants of the mountain, but could not drive out the inhabitants of the valley because they had chariots of iron. (Judges 1:19)

Our victory is in His presence, but when we try to battle out of the wilderness OURSELVES, we are destroyed. We want to be consumed but not destroyed. Esther provides a good example for us to follow. She humbled herself and required nothing (Esther 2:15). The king's presence brings death, but he gave her life and release of his kingdom. May our eyes be lifted off of ourselves and placed upon Jesus - our King.

4. BLOWN UP:
- Your image
- Your ministry
- Your callings

The middle letter of sin is "I." It is also the first letter of IDOLATRY. This is what the Lord wants utterly destroyed in our lives. To envision the meaning of this word, consider this acrostic:

I-mages
D-escribing
O-ther than what the
L-ord
A-ffirms is
T-he
R-eal
Y-ou

Any image we have of ourselves that is NOT GOD'S IMAGE of and in us is an IDOL, a false God. God will not have any other gods before His face (literally). If we face Him in another image (ours/flesh), it is an abomination. Another attribute of the flesh-man, often alluded to by individuals in the third or fourth step, which must be blown up is PERFORMANCE. Performance is the flesh counterfeit to godly obedience. A picture of this is prophetically typed in the second book of the Chronicles. The books of the Chronicles give God's viewpoint to history.

> And now ye think to withstand the kingdom of the Lord in the hand of the sons of David; and ye be a great multitude, and there are with you golden calves, which Jeroboam made you for gods. (II Chronicles 13:8)

The Kingdom of God rests in the hands of the sons of David (true worshipers in spirit and truth), but look who opposes it: "A PEOPLE with GOLDEN CALVES, WHICH JEROBOAM MADE YOU FOR GODS." The name Jeroboam means "struggler." We see the following revelation:

    a. Those who struggle with their own image cause a "golden calf" (IDOL) to be created.

    b. They are now IDOLATERS - and become false gods.

    c. They actually oppose the Kingdom of God coming to themselves in glory.

Destruction of idolatry brings a change from my life, way, and ministry to His life, way, and ministry.

5. BLOWN UP:

- Religious works
- Religious sacrifices

Religion will run you in circles before it kills you! This is what the veil (Lot) did to Abram. It kept him going in circles until it was removed. Also, religion brings DECEPTION to you and me. Deception will cause us to walk in:

- Doctrines and more doctrines.
- Traditions galore.
- Secret sins.
- Disobedience to truth.

Paul warns Timothy about the deception of religious flesh. He told him such individuals are, "always learning but never able to come to the knowledge of the truth," and they "have a form (image) of godliness but deny the power thereof: from such turn away" (II Timothy 3:7, 5). Jesus also declared that religious traditions made the gospel of no effect (Mark 7:13).

- Your feelings
- Your judgments
- Your opinions

This is the final area of the flesh-man's nature from this text. It is best illustrated by the sheep/goat scenario. The goats are always but... ting:

- "But, I feel this way..."
- "But, She did that wrong..."
- "But, I don't see that..."

Jesus said that He would separate the sheep from the goats. We have not realized this "goat nature" of the flesh is in some of us: hence, our need for deliverance in the wilderness. People with goat natures are basically trouble makers. They never really agree on the inside, even though they wear a mask (veil) on their face. People, having been dealt with by God in this area, are transformed into peacemakers. Peter, James and John are good examples of the before/after dealings of God in this area. Before, they were like a BOMB, wanting to call fire down on Samaria (Luke 9:54). After, they were like a BALM, releasing healing to a man at the gate beautiful (Acts 3:3-8). What a difference!

7. RELEASED:
- God's revelation
- God's direction
- God's plans
- God's honor
- God's image
- God's works
- God's heart
- God's judgments
- The glory of the Kingdom

What a deliverance! From the *in part* realm of mixture and duality, to a realm of completeness

What a deliverance! From the *in part* realm of mixture and duality, to a realm of completeness and singleness. We are coming to a fresh understanding of what it means to delight ourselves in the Lord. Note the 58th chapter of Isaiah, verses 13 and 14. They reveal that delighting in Him means to:

- NOT do our own thing.
- NOT find our own pleasures.
- NOT speak our own words.

When we delight ourselves in our deliverance from the flesh-man; we will automatically desire to do God's will, please Him, and speak His words. Our reward, the heritage of Jacob (flesh), now Israel (spirit), is to enjoy the high places (the Most Holy Place - heavenlies) of God! As Isaiah aptly states, "Arise, shake thyself from the dust [flesh-man], and sit down [in my throne-in the Most Holy Place]" (Isaiah 52:2). The mystery is that this glory is to be manifested through God's temple - YOU and ME!

For further study concerning the dealings of God, I suggest two additional key texts, providing this present truth reality of "7-7-7" in our lives:

Text one: Seven churches in Revelation with their dealings/promises (Revelation 2 and 3).

Text two: Seven seals in Revelation with their dealings/promises (Revelation 6 and 8).

CHAPTER TWELVE

MYSTERY OF THE SCROLLS

The word "revelation" is defined as an unveiling, or revealing. This revelation of Jesus is not in heaven, but in US! We realize the perfect when it comes is NOT the scripture, but Jesus manifested in all His glory IN THE SAINTS.

I also want to mention the seventh ANGEL and the seventh TRUMP. As we enter the seventh generation from Adam we hear the seventh trump of God in the earth declaring the results of the wilderness adventure:

> But in the days of the voice of the seventh angel, when he shall begin to sound, the mystery of God should be finished, as He hath declared to his servants the prophets. And the voice which I heard from heaven spake unto me again, and said, "Go and take the little book which is open in the hand of the angel which standeth upon the sea and upon the earth." And I went unto the angel, and said unto him, "Give me the little book." And he said unto me, "Take it, and eat it up; and it shall make thy belly bitter, but it shall be in thy mouth sweet as honey." And I took the little book out of the angel's hand, and ate it up; and it was in my mouth sweet as honey: and as soon as I had eaten it, my belly was bitter. And he said unto me, "Thou must prophesy again before many peoples, and nations, and tongues, and kings. (Revelation 10:7-11)
>
> And the seventh angel sounded; and there were great voices in heaven, saying, "The kingdoms of this world are become the

kingdoms of our Lord, and of his Christ; and he shall reign for ever and ever. (Revelation 11:15)

Then said I, "Lo, I come (in the volume of the book it is written of me,) to do Thy will, O God." (Hebrews 10:7)

Forasmuch as ye are manifestly declared to be the epistle of Christ ministered by us, written not with ink, but with the Spirit of the living God; not in tables of stone, but in fleshly tables of the heart. (II Corinthians 3:3)

And I saw in the right hand of Him that sat on the throne a book written within and on the back side, sealed with seven seals. And I saw a strong angel proclaiming with a loud voice, "Who is worthy to open the book, and to loose the seals thereof?" And no man in heaven, nor in earth, nor under the earth, was able to open the book, neither to look thereon. And I wept much, because no man was found worthy to open and to read the book, neither to look thereon...And I beheld, and, lo, in the midst of the throne, and of the four beasts, and in the midst of the elders, stood a Lamb as it had been slain, having seven horns and seven eyes, which are the seven Spirits of God sent forth into all the earth. And he came and took the book out of the right hand of him that sat upon the throne...And I saw when the lamb opened one of the seals, and I heard, as it were the noise of thunder, one of the four beasts saying, "Come and see." (Revelation 5:1-4, 6-7; 6:1)

These verses begin to reveal the mystery (sacred secrets) of the scrolls (which means books, epistles, or letters). Here are the important points of note:

1. The book is NOT the Bible.
2. The "little book" eaten is the revelation of the Christ.
3. This revelation is released in the wilderness, as bitterness to the stomach (carnal/flesh) but sweetness to the taste (spirit/revelation i.e. "honey").
4. The "kingdoms of this world" (flesh life) have become (are consumed by) the "kingdoms of our Lord" Jesus and His Christ (us); hence, the Adam bomb.
5. The seventh trumpet sounds the end of the mystery, as it is now revealed, **"Christ in you, the hope of glory."**
6. Jesus is NOT the book.
7. WE are the book.
8. Jesus is the only one worthy to open the seals of the book because He paid the price for our dealings.
9. In the volume of the book, it is written of me. The revelation of the Christ is in the book.
10. We are called to prophesy and release the revelation of the Christ in others.
11. The completion of the mystery brings us into the Most Holy Place with its Feast of Tabernacles. This is where the Kingdom of God will flow out of us as king/priests before our God. Awesome! This gives added meaning to the verse in John that tells us the "Word was made flesh..." (John 1:14). This unique experience in the wilderness has been ordained to release the King and His Kingdom, where two natures (kingdoms) are now becoming one.

CHAPTER THIRTEEN

AS HE IS - I AM!

*I*t is the dawning of a new day! The old prophetic order of Eli (spiritually blind) is making room for the Samuel order of prophets. This new prophetic order will prophesy and declare a rending (cutting off) of the old king (Saul/flesh) and his kingdom (flesh nature). The old king will be replaced by the King of Kings, Jesus of Nazareth, and the divine nature of the Kingdom of God.

As we move from glory to glory, we leave the Holy Place with its baptism of the Spirit and its accompanying wilderness. We are stepping into another realm in God with some fresh emphasis including:

1. Baptism of fire.
2. Union versus unity.
3. Singleness versus duality.
4. Perfection or maturity versus hanging in there.
5. Ministering versus always needing ministry.
6. Mind of Christ versus carnal mind.
7. Being His will versus doing His will.
8. Ministry of the glory of the Kingdom of God.
9. A glory-filled church.

What an exciting hour to live in! God is calling us to be Him in the earth, manifesting the Son of God to the world. Two familiar verses we want to repeat again:

> But we all, with open face beholding as in a glass the glory of the Lord, are changed into

the same image from glory to glory, even as by the spirit of the Lord. (II Corinthians 3:18)

Because as He is, so are we in this world. (I John 4:17b)

As we yield our lives to the dealings of God seen in:

> Fire ------------------- Father
> Sword ---------------- Word (Son)
> Glass/Mirror ------- Spirit reflecting Jesus

something supernatural, miraculous, and glorious begins to happen. We don't just do things FOR God anymore, or just take actions WITH God, but we walk AS God, demonstrating and manifesting His nature, grace, and glory in the earth.

This is what the Father has long been waiting for, a company of sons in His image, manifesting His glory. The glory being manifested will draw people to God. It is people seeing HIM, and NOT YOU when they look at you. God is preparing hearts to receive Him, beholding His glory in your face! Who is the REAL man in the mirror? Is it me or is it Jesus? The two have become one. As He is - I am!

CHAPTER FOURTEEN

THE EDEN OF GOD

We want to continue our revelatory understanding of the call to be the Christ (anointed
ones) in the earth. This scripture text has
revelatory impact upon our Christian walk and
ministry. (This is not the garden in Genesis.)

> A garden enclosed is my sister, my
> spouse; a spring shut up, a fountain sealed.
> Thy plants are an orchard of pomegranates,
> with pleasant fruits; camphire, with
> spikenard, spikenard and saffron; calamus
> and cinnamon, with all trees of frank-
> incense; myrrh and aloes with all the chief
> spices: A fountain of gardens, a well of
> living waters, and streams from Lebanon.
> Awake, O north wind; and come, thou
> south; blow upon my garden, that the
> spices thereof may flow out. Let my beloved
> come into his garden, and eat his pleasant
> fruits. I am come into my garden, my sister,
> my spouse: I have gathered my myrrh with
> my spice; I have eaten my honeycomb with
> my honey; I have drunk my wine with my
> milk: eat, O friends; drink, yea, drink
> abundantly, O beloved. (Song of Solomon
> 4:12-5:1)

Look at the wealth of revelation the Lord gives
us:
1. We (individually/corporately) are a garden
   of God, i.e. Eden.
2. We are enclosed (veiled).

3. We are a fountain of living waters sealed (inactivated).
4. We have all nine fruits and nine gifts resident within (nature of Jesus).
5. It takes a prophetic/apostolic activation of the Holy Spirit to release a flow of our giftings/ministries.
6. Jesus is the first one to partake of His fruit/gifts in you for His own pleasure.
7. Jesus gives you and me to each other and to the world to partake of Himself through.

Remember who the book is, who is inside it, and who opens it. Here Jesus, through the apostolic/prophetic mantles, releases the revelation of the Christ in us. Jesus removes the seven seals/veils of flesh covering our lives, in order that His LIFE might flow out. The glory of the Kingdom is released, bringing us behind the veil to BE CHRIST in the earth.

UNIT IV
THE FIVE - FACETED GLORY OF GOD

CHAPTER FIFTEEN

THE GLORY - A FRESH LOOK

What is the glory of God? For our understanding, the term "glory of God" has an altogether unique meaning. The "glory of God" means: A manifestation (or unveiling) of God in the earth (you and me). The term anointing is generally correct when used to describe the glory of God, but since we want to show more specific attributes of God's character and expression, anointing will not be used. Another term that we won't use is manifested presence. It is also limiting for the scope of God's character that we want to portray. So, what is the purpose of the glory of God? Simply put, the glory of God transforms our likeness/image into His. His glory is five-faceted:

1. **THE GLORY OF HIS NATURE.**
2. **THE GLORY OF HIS WORD.**
3. **THE GLORY OF HIS POWER.**
4. **THE GLORY OF HIS PRESENCE.**
5. **THE GLORY OF HIS KINGDOM.**

We remember from the story of Moses, God telling him that no man could face the total (Shekinah) glory of God and live. Therefore, God gives it to us in installments, allowing our death (actually our salvation) to be a process. Remember, our salvation and Christian walk is progressive. We find ourselves back in the tabernacle, where the five-faceted glory of God dwells:

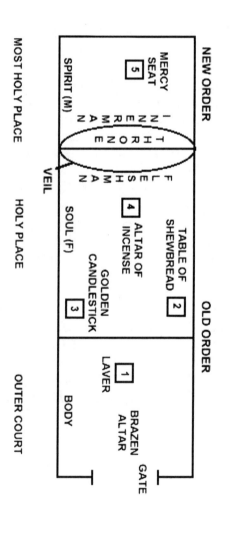

NEW ORDER

OLD ORDER

MOST HOLY PLACE

HOLY PLACE

OUTER COURT

MERCY SEAT

5

SPIRIT (M)

INNERMAN

THEINNER

VEIL

FLESHMAN

SOUL (F)

4 ALTAR OF INCENSE

TABLE OF SHEWBREAD 2

GOLDEN CANDLESTICK 3

1 LAVER

BRAZEN ALTAR

BODY

GATE

The Most Holy Place	Holy Place	Outer Court
Feast of Tabernacles	Feast of Pentecost	Feast of Passover
Baptism in Fire	Baptism in Holy Spirit	Baptism in Water
100-fold	60-fold	30-fold
Third day	Second day	First day
Zion	Philistia	Egypt
Kingdom	Flesh	World
Son	Youth	Babe

Every place in the scripture where the Lord speaks about the glory, the same numerical number pops up! It is the number 120. Every time there is a manifestation of the glory of God, there is a progressive devastation of the flesh-man in our lives. The number 120 is the number for God's glory, and is purposed to end all flesh. As God increases in our lives, we must decrease. The life of self must yield to the life of the divine.

CHAPTER SIXTEEN

THE GLORY OF HIS NATURE

*T*he first place I saw the glory of God revealed was in the account of Noah. We find the numerical type in Genesis 6:3:

> And the Lord said, "My spirit shall not always strive with man, for that he also is flesh: yet his days shall be 120 years."

For our spiritual understanding, the end of all flesh is indicated by the number 120. In the story of Noah, all flesh of sinful man perished, except Noah and his family. The earth was cleansed/purged by a baptism of water. In like fashion, after spiritual death at the brazen alter, we come to the water of the brazen laver. The laver represents washing/cleansing by water. The Bible declares that we are cleansed by the "washing of water by the word" (Ephesians 5:26). Here we find **THE GLORY OF HIS NATURE** involving:

1. Death to the unregenerate spirit.
2. Life-giving water to regenerate the spirit.
3. Death to a godless perspective.
4. Hope in the God of all creation.
5. Death to Satan in our spirit as father.
6. Life in our spirits, through Jesus Christ our Savior.

CHAPTER SEVENTEEN

THE GLORY OF HIS WORD

*T*his aspect of the glory of God coincides with the table of Shewbread, as Jesus (Word) is the "Bread of Life." This is revealed to us in the following account of Moses. Moses received the laws (commandments) of God, written on tablets of stone by the finger of God. These laws (God's Word) provided principles to govern how men were to live with God and one another, but we see Moses' life in the flesh, with God's subsequent dealings, highlighted by the number 120:

> And the Lord said unto him, "This is the land which I swear unto Abraham, unto Isaac, and unto Jacob, saying, 'I will give it unto thy seed': I have caused thee to see it with thine eyes, but thou shalt not go over thither." And Moses was 120 years old when he died: His eye was not dim nor his natural force abated. (Deuteronomy 34:4,7)

From the text, we note a sentence of death is given to Moses' flesh-man by the Word of God. Even though Moses saw the promised land, he still could not enter in. The glory of His Word brought an end to Moses' flesh. **THE GLORY OF HIS WORD** will bring:

1. Death to our worldly standards.
2. Life to godly standards/principles.
3. Death to a life rooted in sin.
4. A sinless life to those rooted in the Word.

CHAPTER EIGHTEEN

THE GLORY OF HIS POWER

*T*he glory of His power is found at the golden candlestick. The golden candlestick with its bowls of oil is representative of the Holy Spirit. The anointing of the Spirit releases **THE GLORY OF HIS POWER** to bring:

1. Death to being changed by will power.
2. Life to being changed by God's power.
3. Death to the fruit of sin.
4. Life to the fruit of the Spirit.
5. Death to ministry by traditions of man.
6. Life to ministry by giftings of the Holy Spirit.

We find the "120" in the upper room waiting and seeking the Lord for His promised power:

> But ye shall receive power, after the Holy Ghost is come upon you: and ye shall be witnesses unto me both in Jerusalem, and all of Judea, and in Samaria, and unto the uttermost part of the earth ...These all continued with one accord in prayer and supplication, with the women, and Mary the mother of Jesus, and with His brethren. And in those days Peter stood up in the midst of the disciples ... (the number of names together were about an hundred and twenty). (Acts 1:8 and 14-15)
>
> And when the day of Pentecost was fully come, they were all with one accord in one place. And suddenly there came a sound from heaven as of a rushing mighty wind, and it filled all the house where they were sitting. And there appeared unto them

cloven tongues like as of fire, and it sat upon each of them. And they were all filled with the Holy Ghost, and began to speak with other tongues, as the Spirit gave them utterance. (Acts 2:1-4)

All the disciples experienced these changes described above, especially our beloved Peter. We readily see the remarkable before/after in Peter's life, as evidenced in the scripture.

CHAPTER NINETEEN

THE GLORY OF HIS PRESENCE

*T*he glory of His presence is located at the alter of incense. This location is special for all Spirit-filled believers as it represents the manifested presence of Jesus by the Holy Spirit. Since we are called to be living sacrifices, it is no longer incense, but praise and worship (fruit of our lips), that invites the glory of His presence.

We find the glory of the "120" expressed beautifully in Solomon's temple:

> Also the Levites which were the singers, all of them of Asaph, of Heman, of Jeduthun, with their sons and their brethren, being arrayed in white linen, having cymbals and psalteries and harps, stood at the east end of the alter, and with them an hundred and twenty priests sounding with trumpets...So that the priests could not stand to minister by reason of the cloud: for the glory of the Lord had filled the house of God. (II Chronicles 5:12, 14)

Here are 120 priests playing 120 trumpets before the Lord. The glory of his Presence was so strong, the priests could not stand up to minister. The cloud of glory filled the house of God. **THE GLORY OF HIS PRESENCE** brings:
1. Death to religious worship.
2. Life to worship by the Spirit.
3. Death to our ministry abilities.
4. Life to His ministry anointings.
5. Death to temporal religious emotion.

6. Life to a heart full of joy in the Holy
   Spirit.

Here we have an interlude which many in the
body of Christ are experiencing. It has been
labeled as the refreshing. It is a fresh release of
the glory of His presence, for those who are or will
be entering the wilderness adventure. It has been
sent by the Lord, in the form of the river, to bring
us into His secret garden (Genesis 2).

The wilderness is also another word to
indicate the "hidden man of the heart." The veil is
there as well, representing the flesh nature. It
must be rent in order to go into the throne room;
the spiritual womb of God; the Kingdom of God;
the Most Holy Place.

CHAPTER TWENTY

THE GLORY OF HIS KINGDOM

*T*he fifth and last unveiling of the glory of God in the earth (ours) is coming upon the Church as we speak. It is represented by the "fiery sword" (the Father and Son coming together) in the wilderness and it is designed to release the last great deliverance in man's soul, conforming him into the image of God. This release of God's glory is also evidenced by the number "120." We find it in the year of jubilee:

> Then shalt thou cause the trumpet of the jubilee to sound on the tenth day of the seventh month, in the day of atonement shall ye make the trumpet sound throughout all your land. And ye shall hallow the fiftieth year, and proclaim liberty throughout all the land unto all the inhabitants thereof: it shall be a jubilee unto you; and ye shall return every man unto his possession, and ye shall return every man unto his family. (Leviticus 25:9-10)

The year of Jubilee signifies freedom, or deliverance from bondage (labors). Jubilee lasts for one full year. It means rest and each one returning to his inheritance. This was to occur every fiftieth year perpetually.

Another "120" clarifies this great event:

It has been "six days" (6,000 years) since Adam. NOW we are coming into the seventh day (year 2000). Fifty years (jubilee) times 120 equals 6,000. We are now coming into the 120th trumpet of jubilee. We are leaving the realm of 6's (flesh), and entering the realm of 7's (perfection / maturity):

- seventh day (from Adam)
- seventh trumpet
- seventh seal

(Review Revelation 10:7-11 and 11:15.)

The five-faceted glory of God that is bringing us into the Kingdom is preparing the Kingdom of God to flow out of you and me. Peter, the apostle, aptly describes the complete process from flesh to glory in I Peter 4:12, 13:

> Beloved, think it not strange concerning the fiery trial which is to try you, as though some strange thing happened unto you: But rejoice, inasmuch as ye are partakers of Christ's sufferings; that, when His glory shall be revealed, ye may be glad also with exceeding joy.

Some additional confirming verses:

> For I reckon that the sufferings of this present time are not worthy to be compared with the glory which shall be revealed in us. (Romans 8:18)
>
> Always bearing about in the body the dying of the Lord Jesus, that the life also of Jesus might be made manifest in our body. For we which live are always delivered unto death for Jesus' sake, that the life also of Jesus might be made manifest in our mortal flesh. So then death worketh in us, but life in you. (II Corinthians 4:10-12)

THE GLORY OF THE KINGDOM brings a great deliverance and:

1. Death to the flesh-man in you.
2. Life to the Christ in you.
3. Death to the carnal mind.
4. Life to the mind of Christ.
5. Death to working with God.
6. Life to ministering as God.
7. Death to the religious order of the flesh in you.
8. Life to the spiritual order of the Kingdom in you.

UNIT V
THE ADMINISTRATION OF GOD'S GLORY

CHAPTER TWENTY-ONE

THE TWO WITNESSES

We have a new order, feast, covenant and government to walk in, or better said, to walk in us. The Most Holy Place is a present reality for us to "live, and move, and have our being..." (Acts 17:28). To confirm and acquaint us clearly with our new posture, God has provided a "cloud of witnesses" in twos:

> This is the third time I am coming to you. In the mouth of two or three witnesses shall every word be established. (II Corinthians 13:1)

The first pair of Kingdom witnesses is found in the ark of the covenant. (The ark is in the sanctuary, the Most Holy Place, and the sanctuary is IN YOU!) Two specific items were added inside the ark, as a potential sign of God's greatness to His people. They were - the golden pot of manna and Aaron's rod that budded.

> And Moses said, "This is the thing which the Lord commanded, 'Fill an omer of it to be kept for your generations; that they may see the bread wherewith I have fed you in the wilderness, when I brought you forth from the land of Egypt.'" And Moses said unto Aaron, "Take a pot, and put an omer full of manna therein, and lay it up before the Lord, to be kept for your generations." As the

Lord commanded Moses, so Aaron laid it up before the Testimony, to be kept. (Exodus 16:32-34)

And it came to pass, that on the morrow Moses, went into the tabernacle of witness; and, behold the rod of Aaron for the house of Levi was budded, and brought forth buds, and bloomed blossoms, and yielded almonds ...And the Lord said unto Moses, "Bring Aaron's rod again before the testimony, to be kept for a token against the rebels; and thou shalt quite take away their murmurings from Me, that they die not." (Numbers 17:8, 10)

And after the second veil, the tabernacle which is called the Holiest of all; which had the golden censer, and the ark of the covenant overlaid round about with gold, wherein was the golden pot that had manna, and Aaron's rod that budded, and the tables of the covenant. (Hebrews 9:3-4)

These two witnesses were placed inside the ark. However, when the ark was brought into the temple of Solomon, after the religious revival under David, something amazing was discovered.

And the priests brought in the ark of the covenant of the Lord unto his place, to the oracles of the house, and into the Most Holy Place, even under the wings of the cherubims...There was nothing in the ark save the two tables which Moses put therein at Horeb, when the Lord made a covenant with the children of Israel, when they came out of Egypt. (II Chronicles 5:7, 10)

The golden pot of manna and Aaron's rod that budded were both missing from the ark. Where did they disappear to? The answer is in the book of Revelation (unveiling).

> He that hath an ear, let him hear what the Spirit saith unto the churches; To him that overcometh will I give to eat of the HIDDEN MANNA, and will give him a white stone, and in the stone a new name written, which no man knoweth saving he that receiveth it ...And he that overcometh, and keepeth My works unto the end, to him will I give power over the nations: And he shall rule them with a ROD OF IRON; as the vessels of a potter shall they be broken to shivers: even as I received of My Father. (Revelation 2:17, 26-27, Emphasis added.)

Both, the hidden manna and the rod that budded are in the hearts and hands of the overcomers. Those who have been "the called" to overcome all flesh, entering behind the veil, will have two witnesses of the Kingdom of God in their lives.

1. The Hidden manna is the ANOINTING to be the revelation of Christ in the earth.
2. Aaron's rod that budded is the AUTHORITY of the rod of iron to walk in the power of the Spirit, with the double portion of king/priest before our God.

We need to realize something important. Jesus unveiled His deity, came to earth, and took on the revelation and veil of man's flesh. Now, we are called to be unveiled of the flesh-man, arise into the heavenlies (Most Holy Place), and take on the revelation of the Christ, the hope of glory. The glory of the Kingdom of God will be visibly seen by a fresh anointing and authority that has not been walked in heretofore.

This brings us to our second pair of witnesses:
1. Authority as KINGS.
2. Anointing as PRIESTS.

This is declared in Revelation: "And [He] hath made us kings and priests unto God and His Father" (Revelation 1:6a).

This is a fresh, new order of things. There were two distinct lines in the Old Testament, the priests and the kings. You were either in a priestly line or possibly a kingly line, but you would never be in both UNTIL NOW.

The third pair of witnesses emerging on the scene today, having true authority and anointing of kings/priests, are the apostles and prophets (Ephesians 4:11). These two mantles work together as the A-R-M of God: to ACTIVATE, RELEASE, and MOBILIZE the Kingdom of God in and through the saints.

> And are built upon the foundation of the APOSTLES and PROPHETS, Jesus Christ Himself being the chief cornerstone. (Ephesians 2:20, emphasis added)
>
> Which in other ages was not made known unto the sons of man, as it is now revealed unto His holy APOSTLES and PROPHETS by the Spirit. (Ephesians 3:5, Emphasis added)

Since we are in a new "third day," with corresponding revelation, feast, baptism, covenant, and anointings, there must be fresh foundations. This charge is given to the mantle of the APOSTLE and PROPHET. They are the foundation stones of the revelation of the Christ and the glory of the Kingdom.

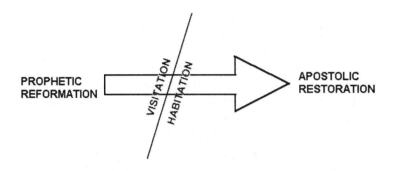

The prophet, with a sword (the Word of the Lord) coming out of his mouth, and the apostle, with the rod of iron in his hand; will be a unified force as forerunners, leading God's people behind the veil into the Kingdom of God (Most Holy Place).They have been ordained by God to exemplify the ANOINTING and AUTHORITY as the two witnesses, preparing a remnant of God's people as kings/priests. The Bible says, "His (God's) ARM shall rule for Him ..." (Isaiah 40:10, Emphasis added). The apostles and the prophets are coming to the forefront, as God's ruling leadership arm. We see this given to us in the I Corinthians:

> And God has set some in the church, first apostles, secondarily prophets, thirdly teachers, after that miracles, then gifts of healings, helps, governments, diversities of tongues. (I Corinthians 12:28)

As the Kingdom of God progresses and enlarges, there will be a change in positional authority. The prophets are now declaring and activating the glory and grace of God. They are also prophesying the release of the apostolic mantle. As the apostolic mantle comes forth, God will realign the prophets to come alongside of the apostles in Kingdom order, "first apostles, secondarily prophets...." We see the practical example from the Antioch church in Acts. The ministry pair were always referred to as Barnabas and Paul. However, when the apostolic anointing was released, the order changed to Paul and Barnabas:

> Which also they did, and sent it to the elders by the hands of Barnabas and Saul...As they ministered to the Lord, and fasted, the Holy Ghost said, Separate me Barnabas and Saul for the work whereunto I have called them...Which was with the deputy of the country, Sergius Paulus, a prudent man; who called for Barnabas and Saul, and desired to hear the word of God...Then Paul and Barnabas waxed bold, and said, "It was necessary that the word of God should first have been spoken to you: but seeing you put it from you, and judge yourselves unworthy of everlasting life, lo, we turn to the Gentiles..." When therefore Paul and Barnabas had no small dissension and disputation with them, they determined that Paul and Barnabas, and certain other of them, should go up to Jerusalem unto the apostles and elders about this question...Then pleased it the apostles and elders, with the whole church, to send

chosen men of their own company to Antioch with Paul and Barnabas; namely, Judas surnamed Barsabas, and Silas, chief men among the brethren...Paul also and Barnabas continued in Antioch, teaching and preaching the word of the Lord, with many others also. (Acts 11:30; 13:2, 7, 46; 15:2, 22, 35)

Then there was Paul (the apostle) and Silas (the prophet), in that order. God has a government called a THEOCRACY. In His theocracy, the ministry leadership in His Church are "FIRST APOSTLES, SECONDARILY PROPHETS, THIRDLY TEACHERS..." (I Corinthians 12:28). This will be the Kingdom order in the move we're entering. It won't be based on western religious traditions, but on the Word and the Kingdom of God. We MUST have new wineskins, individual and corporate, to hold the new wine of His glory and grace that is coming forth.

CHAPTER TWENTY-TWO

AFTER THE ORDER OF MELCHISEDEC

*T*he apostles and prophets will release the new order of king/priests, with its pattern (as Jesus Himself patterned it) "after the order of Melchisedec" (Hebrews 6:20). I believe Melchisedec was a Christopheny (Jesus incarnated in human flesh in the Old Testament). The scripture tends to support this assertion as it details Melchisedec's roots.

> Without father, without mother, without descent, having neither beginning of days, nor end of life; but made like unto the Son of God; abideth a priest continually. (Hebrews 7:3)

Melchisedec was the king of Salem and a priest of the most high God. (Genesis 14:18). He is the spiritual type for our kingship/priesthood. He blessed and served Abram "bread and wine" (Genesis 14:18-19). Look what he served Abram:
1. Bread - the ANOINTING of the WORD ("hidden manna").
2. Wine - the AUTHORITY of the SPIRIT ("rod of iron").

This new order has fresh, significant meaning for us. (Remember, the Kingdom of God is WITHIN YOU (Luke 17:21).
    a. Our new flow will be OUT of the Most Holy Place. The Kingdom of God will be flowing out of US to others

Afterward he brought me again unto the door of the house; and, behold, waters issued out from under the threshold of the house eastward: for the forefront of the house stood toward the east, and the waters came down from under from the right side of the house, at the south side of the altar. (Ezekiel 47:1)

b. As we have gazed upon Him who is the mercy seat, we become a seat of mercy; "As He is, so are we in this world" (I John 4:17b). The highest form of worship that we can give to something is to BECOME IT!

c. We will no longer continually look for ministry since we will have become ministry!

d. As Christ in the earth, we king/priests serve Him in word (bread) and spirit (wine) to others.

In addition to the new order, we also have a new covenant. Melchisedec was the king of Salem (which became Jerusalem). Jerusalem means habitation of peace. As we leave the feast of Pentecost, coming through the wilderness veil of the flesh, we enter the Feast of Tabernacles in the Most Holy Place. This feast signifies an indwelling or HABITATION.

This is where apostolic anointing begins to rule, mobilizing the saints into a habitation of peace. This is God's eternal covenant of peace. This is different, because we no longer WORK up the anointing with sweat (Ezekiel 44:8). We now walk in an anointing that ABIDES. This peace releases the Sabbath rest of God, causing us to cease from all earthly/religious toils. We enter His rest and His work.

We embrace His third everlasting covenant, signifying the last phase of the Kingdom, being established upon earth as it is in heaven. The first covenant was the covenant of water. This coincides with the outer court and the glory of His nature demonstrated by the washing of the water by the word and the baptism of water at the brazen laver. God gave Noah this everlasting covenant of water, signified by the rainbow (Genesis 9:12-13).

The second covenant is in the inner court of the Feast of Pentecost. It is the covenant of circumcision. It was given to Abraham, bringing us the spiritual truths (Leviticus 12:3):

1. Done to all males on the eighth day ("new beginnings").
2. Foreskin cut off by a sword (flesh by Word of the Lord).
3. An unveiling to expose the reproductive organ (able to reproduce God's glory and grace entering behind the veil).

Now, coming fully into the third day Feast of Tabernacles within the Most Holy Place, we experience the third everlasting covenant.

Thus saith the Lord, 'The people which were left of the sword found grace in the wilderness; even Israel, when I went to cause him to rest'. (Jeremiah 31:2)

Moreover I will make a covenant of peace with them; it shall be an everlasting covenant with them: and I will place them, and multiply them, and will set My sanctuary in the midst of them forever more. My tabernacle also shall be with them: yea, I

will be there God, and they shall be my
people. And the heathen shall know that I
the Lord do sanctify Israel, for My sanctuary
shall be in the midst of them for evermore.
(Ezekiel 37:26-28)

As the guard changes and we leave the old
order to embrace the new, we will manifest this
new everlasting covenant, signifying our walk as
kings/priests before God. These verses prophetically tell us:

1. After the sword in the wilderness (flesh-
   man consumed by the fiery sword) the
   grace of the Lord (that reproduces and
   brings us behind the veil) causes us to
   rest.
2. God will place His sanctuary in the midst
   of you, individually and corporately, as His
   Most Holy Place.
3. He will set or establish the Kingdom of
   God in and through you.
4. He will reproduce and multiply Himself
   through you.
5. The world will recognize God, as He causes
   the glory of the Kingdom to be seen arising
   from us, individually and corporately.

Therefore, God is dealing, moving, and confirming His progressive will in and through us by
two witnesses:

1. Word/Spirit
2. Hidden manna/rod that budded
3. King/priests
4. Apostle/Prophet

The dawning of a new day is bringing fresh:

   a. Revelation - Christ in you...Glory of the
      Kingdom (in you).

b. Anointings - Kingly/Priestly ministry Ministry of the glory.
c. Doctrinal focus - grace of God, glory of God, baptism of fire, Melchisedec priesthood, covenant of peace, union (instead of unity) perfection realm, Kingdom of God, and BE versus DO.

The end-time company of apostles and prophets have a powerful charge from the Lord. They are to mobilize the people of God into a mighty army, demonstrating His glory and power in the earth. This process, the prophetic reformation along with apostolic habitation, will occur prior to the ministry of RECONCILIATION. The ministry of reconciliation will take place as the glory of the Lord exudes from the saints of God, causing multitudes to flock to the saving knowledge of Jesus Christ. This last great outpouring of His glory through the saints in the streets, reconciling the lost to Himself, will climax in the personal, bodily return of Jesus of Nazareth to planet earth.

Prior to His personal return, one evident sign through the apostolic rule will be the FEAR of the LORD. The anointing and authority of God demonstrated through the apostolic/prophetic company will not be childish, fleshy, or something to be discarded and rejected. The biblical story of Ananias and Sapphira in the book of Acts (of the Holy Spirit through the disciples), gives us a graphic reminder that God doesn't play religious games.

Read Acts chapter 5, verses 3-11 to get fresh perspective of this authority being restored to the church of Jesus Christ.

CHAPTER TWENTY-THREE

THE MINISTRY OF GOD'S GLORY

We want to turn our attention to prophetic revelation and principles, involving the release of God's glory in the local churches. A fresh new DELIVERANCE is coming. It is not the old order of "come out you devil" (which is still needed in the maturation process). It is deliverance by the FIRE/SWORD of the Lord out of the flesh nature, and into the divine nature (spirit, now soul). This is NOT a removal of spirits, but a change in NATURE! What is the immediate fruit of this deliverance by the glory of the Kingdom? Here are some practical thoughts:

1. A new found freedom/reality that says to us - we don't have TO SIN anymore.
2. The awesome awareness of the personal reality of Jesus as our Lord and King.
3. The realization that the Kingdom of God IS IN YOU.
4. Our focus moving from doing (Martha), to being (Mary).
5. Our ministry is no longer for Jesus, or with Jesus, but AS JESUS.

We are going to two specific events in scripture, giving us revelatory understanding of our fresh new walk of ministry unto God. First is the story of the resurrection of Lazarus. It is found in John, the eleventh chapter. I won't quote the bulk of the chapter, but give you prophetic insights with corresponding verses:

1. Resurrection life from dead flesh comes in the third day (Allowing one day for the messenger plus THREE DAYS for Jesus to

show up in Bethany equals four days that Lazarus was dead) (John 11:3, 6, 17)

2. Jesus spoke the creative word to release the glory and life. (The mouthpiece of the Lord (apostolic/prophetic) speaks and releases the glory and life. (John 11:43).

3. Lazarus' flesh was bound in three ways (John 11:44). His eyes were covered with a napkin (veil), also his hands and feet were bound. Note the bondage "strips" of the flesh:
   a. eyes with napkin (veil) - lust of the eyes
   b. hands (works) - lust of the flesh
   c. feet (walk) - pride of life

These are the manifestations of the flesh-man. We want to understand how these have manifested in the Church, individually and corporately:

- individually:
   a. Lust of the eyes - vain expectations.
   b. Lust of the flesh - spiritual requirements.
   c. Pride of life - performance love.
- corporately (i.e. Laodicean Church):
   a. Lust of the eyes - "come hear our beautiful choir."
   b. Lust of the flesh - "fastest growing church in town."
   c. Pride of life - "programs for everyone from the cradle to the grave."

It takes the prophetic word as eye salve, to open the blind (veiled) eyes, along with the sword wielded to cut off the bondage to the work of our hands. It involves a joint prophetic/apostolic anointing, releasing the GLORY of the KINGDOM with its mighty deliverance from death unto life.

4. Jesus said unto them, "Loose him and let him go" (John 11:44). The ministry of the glory of the Kingdom is to be released and given to the body in order to activate the lives of others. It is not to remain a ministry of the few.

Let us look at a few practical tips concerning this ministry to others:

1. John 11:3 - Jesus didn't look for people to release His ministry unto. They came to Him. God will send people your way! They will cross your path when least expected.

2. John 11:41-42 - People in need will come to the anointing. Don't press people for your ministry, but press into God for the anointing.

3. John 11:6 - Don't be harassed to minister quickly, because God has a perfect time for His will to be accomplished.

4. John 11:44; Isaiah 65:8 - The ministry doesn't all depend upon you. It is the glory of God for a team of ministers to release the glory of the Kingdom.

5. John 11:40 - Believing and trusting God is what releases the glory of God. (A quiet confidence, allowing Him to have His way.)

Jesus knew who He was, and was secure in His Father's love and will. We too, must be secure (not jealous, competitive, or defensive), knowing the Father's love, being confident of Him who is mighty within us to save and deliver.

The second event in scripture is recorded in John 5:2-9. (Since the text is loaded with revelatory insight, we will quote the whole section, giving points of prophetic application):

Now there is at Jerusalem by the sheep market a pool, which is called in the Hebrew tongue Bethesda, having five porches. In these lay a great multitude of impotent folk, of blind, halt, withered, waiting for the moving of the water. For an angel went down at a certain season into the pool, and troubled the water: whosoever then first after the troubling of the water stepped in was made whole of whatsoever disease he had. And a certain man was there, which had an infirmity thirty and eight years. When Jesus saw him lie, and knew that he had been now a long time in that case, He saith unto him, 'Wilt thou be made whole?' The impotent man answered him, 'Sir, I have no man, when the water is troubled, to put me into the pool: but while I am coming, another steppeth down before me.' Jesus saith unto him, 'Rise, take up thy bed and walk.' And immediately the man was made whole, and took up his bed, and walked: and on the same day was the Sabbath.

1. Pool:
   a. Called Bethesda meaning "house of mercy." We are being called to Him who sits upon the mercy seat in the Most Holy Place. In so doing, we are becoming a house of mercy.
   b. It has 5 (five) porches. Five is the number for the GRACE of God. The grace of God brings us into the waters of life, in order to bring forth healing to the nations.

   c. Five is also the number of the five-fold ministry of Ephesians 4:11, apostle, prophet, evangelist, pastor and teacher.

2. Great multitude - a lot of church people (sheep) wandering around.

3. They had 5 (five) conditions:

   a. Impotent – They have no power or strength, and no ability to reproduce. Those people had no divine life flow, nor did they have the power to reproduce Him.

   b. Blind – They are not able to see (have a vision) or see clearly (blur/veil). Many were blinded by their traditions, which made the gospel of no effect!

   c. Halt – They are standing still and not going forward. They remained in the old order, and had become legal (wouldn't change).

   d. Withered – They are dried up from lack of use. No fresh anointing of the Word to exercise the muscles of faith.

   e. Waiting – They are always looking for another meeting to go to in order to get a blessing, instead of going to a meeting in order to BE A BLESSING!

4. God has given the five-fold ministry to bring restoration to these conditions:

   a. IMPOTENT - APOSTLES (foundational) - They declare and release the glory of the Kingdom, the glory of His presence; in order to release deliverance by the divine life-flow of the Christ, and the grace to reproduce His life in others.

   b. BLIND - PROPHETS (foundational) – They declare and release the glory of the Kingdom/the glory of His presence, the veil (flesh - no vision), bringing forth the revelation of the Christ in you, the hope of glory.

c. HALT - PASTORS (shepherds) - the glory of His nature – They lovingly and gently leading the sheep into "green pastures" (revelation word of apostles and prophets), and beside the "still waters" (practical experiences of the Holy Spirit in their lives and in their midst).

d. WITHERED - TEACHERS (not "Sunday School" teachers) - the glory of His Word – They provide application of the revelation word in order to exercise the muscles (faith and ministry) of the sheep.

e. WAITING - EVANGELIST - releasing the glory of His power – They are anointed to release the blessings of His power (gifts of the Spirit); They assist apostles and prophets as they ground others in the basics of Spirit-filled living, reproducing new lambs of God.

5. Certain seasons - indicates major restorations with its various movements:

a. Feast of Passover restored:

    1. Salvation - evangelical movement (various doctrines)

        a. Born-again experience

        b. Baptism in water

        c. Sanctification

b. Feast of Pentecost restored - Spirit-filled Pentecostal and Charismatic movements.

(Various doctrines)
1. Baptism in the Holy Spirit
2. Tongues
3. Healings/miracles/deliverance
4. Five-fold ministry
5. Gifts/fruit of the Spirit
6. Faith
7. Unity
8. Praise/Worship
9. Prophetic ministry
10. Feast of Tabernacles restored -
11. Perfection - Kingdom movement
    (Various doctrines)
    a. Manifested sonship
    b. King/Priests
    c. Baptism in fire
    d. The glory of God
    e. Overcomers
    f. The sovereignty of God
    g. Union
    h. Apostolic ministry
    i. Covenant of peace - Sabbath rest

6. Troubled waters - the moves of the Holy Spirit in the local church, regional area, or in various parts of the world. When the Spirit moves, things will happen.
7. Certain man - any man/woman of the multitude (church or churches) - could be YOU.
8. Thirty-eight years - from the charismatic movement to the kingdom movement.
9. "I have no man..." - two perspectives:
   a. Sincere -true cry of a heart wanting more of the things of God.
   b. Religious - selfish and self-centered - complaint of one who says everybody gets ministry but me.

10. "Rise" - the mouthpiece of the Lord speaks and imparts divine life flow.
11. "Take up your bed" - the activation to reproduce divine life.
12. "Walk" - release to be led by the Spirit (as a mature son-the Greek huios) of God.

What we have is the reality of the five-fold ministry, led by the apostolic and prophetic foundational ministries, releasing the glory of the Kingdom in and through God's people. As the mystery is released, the people of God will say, "I AM THE MAN! Step down into MY waters and receive of Him." We will have become the manifestation of the sons of God, manifesting the Son of God.

CHAPTER TWENTY-FOUR

SAVIORS ON MOUNT ZION

As we continue to gain understanding of the revelation of our ministry of the glory, I want to focus clearly on our true identity. This is what the flesh-man is veiling over our faces. He knows that his unveiling will be his undoing. Therefore, he hinders the sons of God from taking their inheritance in the Kingdom (II Thessalonians 2:7 - he who now "letteth" [means hinders] is NOT the Holy Spirit - but the MAN of FLESH.)

Our inheritance of the Kingdom of God is prophetically given to us in the book of Obadiah.

> But upon mount Zion shall be deliverance, and there shall be holiness; and the house of Jacob shall possess their possessions. And the house of Jacob shall be a fire, and the house of Joseph a flame, and the house of Esau for stubble, and they shall kindle in them, and devour them; and there shall not be any remaining of the house of Esau; for the Lord hath spoken it...And saviors shall come up on mount Zion to judge the mount of Esau; and the kingdom shall be the Lord's. (Obadiah 17, 18, 21)

These are the prophetic declarations concerning our posture and position:
1. "Zion" is the people of God.
2. "Deliverance" means the end of all flesh.
3. "Holiness" is the fruit of a walk cleansed of all "filthiness of FLESH and spirit."

4. "Shall possess their possessions" We shall not only be in the Kingdom, but the Kingdom be in us.
5. "House of Jacob" is now the Israel of God, because she prevailed.
6. "Shall be a fire" indicates that the baptism of fire shall be in her midst.
7. "House of Joseph - a flame" Joseph is a son of Jacob. You and I are a type of Joseph (one member of the body). Joseph was a flame. He became the fire. You and I also are becoming the fire.
8. "Esau for stubble" The Esau nature (flesh-man) now becomes the substance to be consumed by fire. Where is the fire? It is in YOU and ME. The Esau nature is being consumed out of our lives.
9. "Shall not be any remaining of the house of Esau" The fire of God shall consume all flesh. We shall no longer walk in two natures but ONE.
10. "Saviors shall come up on mount Zion" Jesus our Deliverer and our Savior has now become IN US a savior to others.
11. "To judge the mounts of Esau" We now execute "righteous judgment" towards the Esau nature. By the anointing of the Word and the authority of the Spirit, we declare, release, and activate the glory of His Kingdom, consuming the flesh-man (Esau nature) in others.
12. "The kingdom shall be the Lord's" The government of God is being established in the hearts/lives of God's people. "The kingdoms of this world are become the kingdoms of our Lord [Jesus] and his Christ [US-anointed ones]. We begin to sense this

awesome posture, as we hear Jesus echo these words to His disciples: "Whose soever sins ye remit, they are remitted unto them; and whose soever sins you retain, they are retained" (John 20:23).

The anointing and authority of the Kingdom will ABIDE in the true disciples of the Lord in this last hour. Beloved, the heaven in you will consume and destroy the hell in others!

CHAPTER TWENTY-FIVE

PRACTICAL MINISTRY TIPS

1. The initial declarations, impartations, and release of the glory of the Kingdom will rest solely upon the shoulders of God's true apostles and prophets.

2. You cannot release the glory unless the glory of the Kingdom has been released in you. The anointing and authority is transferred from the apostolic/prophetic mantle.

3. This fresh deliverance of the fiery sword comes out of the EYES and the MOUTH. You don't have to lay hands on them to release it.

4. After the ministry of the glory of His Kingdom has been released, then impartation of God's grace and anointings can be activated with the laying on of hands.

5. Manifestations may vary, but the primary one observed is God's covenant of peace. EACH ONE WILL REALLY KNOW THAT THEY ARE IN THE KINGDOM, AND THEY WILL KNOW THE PRESENT REALITY THAT THE KINGDOM OF GOD IS WITHIN THEM.

6. This is NOT a deliverance of demonic spirits, activated through the gifts of the Spirit. It is a deliverance involving a CHANGE of NATURE. It is activated and released by the fire of God in the eyes and the sword of the Lord in the mouth. No commands spoken to demons are appropriate during this special ministry time, unless a clear indication is warranted, and acknowledgment given by leadership.

7. This ministry is overseen by the Lord Himself so that others will seek, ask for, and yield

to the Lord for this ministry. You are not to offer it to those just wanting a sip.

CHAPTER TWENTY-SIX

QUESTIONS AND ANSWERS

1.Q: Is the "refreshing" and the ministry of the glory of the Kingdom the same thing?

A: No. The real purpose of the *river of refreshing* is to carry who the Lord is drawing into the wilderness adventure. It prepares the heart for the secret garden and the glory of the Kingdom.

2.Q: Exactly where is the wilderness?

A: The wilderness is just this side of the veil of the flesh, located in the Holy Place of the soul.

3.Q: Where is the heart of man?

A: The heart, or inner man, is the union of man's soul and spirit.

4.Q: Where is the heart of man in relation to the veil?

A: It actually contains the veil (flesh) until the veil is rent. This is why we are a mixture (dual), with carnal/divine natures, until the veil is rent. Then we go behind the veil (still in the heart area of the Most Holy Place), into the throne room of God. This is also the spiritual WOMB of God, where He reproduces Himself through us.

5.Q: I thought my "old man" died at salvation.

A: If he did, what is the problem now? The answer is that he isn't experientially dead yet. Positionally he is, but our salvation is progressive. Therefore, God is bringing a total death to the man of flesh, in order that the man of the Spirit can come forth.

6.Q: What is the basic difference between the flesh and a demon?

A: The flesh is a nature, but a demon is a spirit. You cannot cast out a nature. All you can do is to cut it off and consume it. A demon cannot be consumed, it must be cast out.

7.Q: Does the revelation in this book tell me that I am God?

A: No, the mystery of Christ in you, the hope of glory, reveals that we BECOME AS GOD (I John 4:17b). This is contrasted with unity from the Holy Place, as we did everything with God.

8.Q: What long range purpose will be served by being AS GOD?

A: The time will come when the world will ask you to show them the Father. You will humbly reply as Jesus- "When you have seen me you have seen the Father."

9.Q: I thought we wouldn't be like Him until He returns.

A: Full restoration of soul/spirit will be unveiled PRIOR to His physical return. This is what the Bible declares in Acts 3:20 – 21:

> And that He may send Jesus, the Christ appointed for you, whom heaven must receive until the period of the restoration of all things about which God spoke by the mouth of His holy prophets from ancient time.

Total redemption won't occur until He returns physically, transforming our mortal bodies (re-read I John 3:2 carefully!).

10.Q: Some say the second day realm is an in part realm, and therefore passed away.

A: The manifestation of Jesus of Nazareth in our lives progressively encompasses every realm, from the first day through the third day. The new order doesn't make the old unnecessary, but adds fresh unveilings of Him in us, "line upon line," providing a complete focus. Though the first and second days are swallowed up into the third; every unveiling is necessary, since God's chosen people are at different places in their walk with Him.

FOUNDATION MINISTRIES

PRODUCT AND MINISTRY INFORMATION

BOOKS

The Unveiling... is available at a cost of $8.95 each, plus $2.00 per copy for shipping and handling. Canadian residents, please remit by postal money order in U.S. funds. Other foreign residents, remit in U.S. dollars or equivalent. Please make your remittance payable to: **Foundation Ministries**.

Contact us about bulk orders of 10 or more.

MINISTRY INFORMATION

For available dates for the ministry of **Monty Stratton**, or further information, please call or write:

FOUNDATION MINISTRIES INTERNATIONAL

8703 GAYTON RD.

RICHMOND, VA 23229

PHONE: (804) 754-3811

E-MAIL: foundationministries@fm-i.org

WEBSITE: www.fm-i.org